SUPPORTING POLICING STUDENTS

More policing titles

Behavioural Skills for Effective Policing: The Service Speaks
Edited by Mark Kilgallon and Martin Wright
ISBN: 9781914171383

Criminology and Crime Prevention
By James Dickety, Edited by Tony Blockley
ISBN: 9781915080745

Critical Thinking Skills for your Policing Degree
By Jane Bottomley, Martin Wright and Steven Pryjmachuk
ISBN: 9781913063450

Dilemmas and Decision Making in Policing
By Emma Spooner and Bob Cooper
ISBN: 9781915713124

Leadership Behaviours for Effective Policing: The Service Speaks
Edited by Mark Kilgallon and Martin Wright
ISBN: 9781915080530

Listening Skills for Effective Policing
By Andy Fairie
ISBN: 9781915713452

The Essential Police Constable Degree Apprenticeship EPA Handbook
By Sharon Gander
ISBN: 9781915080714

Routledge
Taylor & Francis Group

LONDON AND NEW YORK

SUPPORTING POLICING STUDENTS

A Handbook for Lecturers, Tutors, Coaches and Mentors

JAMES DICKETY

Cover design by Out of House Limited

First published in 2025 by Routledge
4 Park Square, Milton Park, Abingdon, Oxon OX14 4RN

and by Routledge
605 Third Avenue, New York, NY 10017

*Routledge is an imprint of the Taylor & Francis Group,
an informa business*

British Library Cataloguing in Publication Data
A CIP record for this book is available from the British Library

ISBN: 9781916925113 (pbk)
ISBN: 9781041057161 (ebk)

DOI: 10.4324/9781041057161

Text design by Greensplash
Typeset in Calibri Regular
by Newgen Publishing UK

CONTENTS

Acknowledgements

I want to start by thanking all those involved in helping to create this title, especially Lily and Julia from Critical Publishing for bringing this book to fruition. Lily has probably played the most important role in making sure this title is both useful and legible!

Secondly, I want to thank my partner, who has listened to me endlessly talking about needing to write this book, while also ensuring I had breaks so I did not burn myself out. She accomplished this while she was pregnant and then a new mum. Managing any one of these is not a simple task.

Finally, I wish to thank all those who have supported me in my career. I will not name you, for obvious reasons, but hopefully you know who you are, and I will forever be indebted to you. These people played a vital role in moulding the officer I have become and the individual I am today – many acting as unofficial parents when I started so young!

I hope this book is of use to you as you guide the police officers of the future, and good luck in whatever role you may have.

Meet the author

James Dickety has worked in policing for fourteen years as a special constable, police constable, a detective within CID and now within investigator development. He has worked on neighbourhood policing teams, response teams, operations and within investigations. His key interest is developing knowledge within the service and bridging the gap between academia and policing. James has a degree in criminology and criminal justice from the University of Portsmouth and has studied at both undergraduate and master's level in policing policy and leadership.

Part 1

Learning theory

Thank you

Starting with a 'thank you' can often seem on the author's part as self-serving in an effort to thank you for purchasing or borrowing this title in the evitable hope of getting others to buy it as well. The reality is, however, that policing is hard and often thankless, and it does not cost much to recognise this. The work done by those in policing is in many cases best described as heroic and is done so despite the intense amount of public scrutiny, which whilst rightly placed upon us, is often lacking balance such as when incidents debated over five-second clips on social media when the incident often has taken place over a far longer period.

Individuals are joining policing at a time when public confidence has been eroded. This is due to several factors including the abhorrent acts of a select few in the service which has understandably tarnished the perception of policing. Policing is also rarely involved in the high points in people's lives. Dare I say that policing does not share the clear image of success other emergency services have, such as the fire service putting out a fire or rescuing a cat from a tree. Within policing you will not know if you have saved a life by locking up a domestic abuse perpetrator and you will not know if your crime prevention advice has prevented another offence, but this does not make this work worthless. In fact, I would argue it makes it even more important to keep going.

Regardless of being involved with what can be the worst part in many people's lives, whether as an officer, staff member or volunteer, your efforts often fail to get the credit they deserve from the public.

Thank yous do not have to be in the form of a certificate or a letter in the post, although they are nice. But it can be an acknowledgement of the toll policing can take on you, the impact of attending countless traumatic incidents or even having to mark the 1,000th essay! Remember every contact you have in some way leaves its mark on you.

As a result, I want to start with a thank you. Whatever your role is in supporting policing students, you are supporting them to enter this often unseen career. Many of you may also be doing 'the job' at the same time, meaning you are balancing your own workload and that of your student. Others will be trying to balance the needs of academia alongside the difficult desire to have officers on the street. This is not easy and without your support, the next generation of officer, PCSO, police staff member or volunteer simply would not exist, and often your work and impact is both underestimated and undervalued, so thank you.

This book intends to help support you in your role of supporting others. Naturally not all of it will be relevant to each and every one of you, all of the time. But the contents of this title are intentionally broad to cover a spectrum of topics which should provide at least some help to you and can be referred to later on. To help assist with this mission, the book is broken up into three sections.

Part 1 focusses on an introduction to coaching, mentoring and learning theory. I know that some in policing may turn their nose up at the idea of theory; however, good practice is often based upon solid theory and research in the topic area at hand. You will find that the later chapters link to the theory, and as such it is helpful context which you should find helps improve your practice.

Part 2 moves its focus towards developing students, whether that be leadership, feedback or performance conversations. These are skills which are often expected from tutors, coaches and educators but in my experience are very rarely discussed. Hopefully from reading these chapters you will find a range of approaches that you can incorporate into your own practice and make these often difficult skills easier.

Finally, Part 3 looks at policing specifics such as dealing with domestic abuse, death, going to court and the National Investigators' Exam (NIE). Some of these areas you may not have dealt with personally, or may not have for some time, but yet you may be expected to support trainees with them! These chapters will have a slightly different tone to help provide you with ideas to guide you through supporting a student so you are not left trying to do your best without at least something to help point you in the right direction.

I hope you find this book useful. Good luck in your endeavours and, as always, thank you.

Part 1

Part 1 is a section I feared writing; whenever you write the word 'theory' I always worry that those in policing typically switch off. That said, however, I hope that with the increasing input of academia in police education this perception may ease.

Theory is vitally important. As a service we are aiming to become increasingly evidence-based and theory is invariably well researched. Even if this research is not in the policing arena, it does not make it irrelevant or worthless to us, and policing can be greatly improved by learning from it.

The first chapter looks at the differences between a mentor and a coach. Despite these terms being frequently used interchangeably in policing, there are some key differences which are important to know, especially if you interact with educators outside of policing.

Chapter 2 takes a more practical look at research and examines what makes a good coach. There has been a range of research in policing, teaching and nursing, all of which would be beneficial to know for your practice. This chapter intends to pull it together so you use it in your setting.

Chapter 3 looks at coaching models. Despite there being a clear distinction between mentoring and coaching, there is not one singular approach to them. This chapter describes some of the key models you could use in your practice and highlight some of the limitations. It will not advocate the use of one model over another; their implementation is personal to both you as the person supporting someone and the scenario in which you are doing so. At the end of this chapter it is hoped that you have enough information to be able to cherry-pick what works for you.

Following the completion of Part 1, it is hoped you will have a good grounding in the broad areas covered by this book, which will lead nicely onto Part 2, which delves into the practicalities.

Chapter 1

WHAT IS THE DIFFERENCE BETWEEN A MENTOR AND A COACH?

LEARNING OBJECTIVES

After reading this chapter you will be able to:

- understand what a coach is;
- understand the role of a mentor;
- recognise the difference between the two roles;
- identify when to use each approach.

Introduction

From personal experience, the terms mentor, tutor, coach, or anything else your force may use, are often confused and used interchangeably not just across forces but also internally. This is understandable given that policing's experience of these roles has been much the same but is also unnecessary and creates confusion such as when transferees move forces and have to learn the new force terminology. It is therefore important to realise that there is a subtle but clear difference and that we must utilise the right language to help everyone involved in the process. We do not want students or colleagues getting confused or misunderstanding what the relationship is. This chapter explains each role and examines their key differences, highlighting appropriate opportunities within policing where you might wish to adopt each role.

REFLECTIVE PRACTICE 1.1

Before this chapter goes further, consider the following.

- What might be the differences between a mentor and a coach?
- Why do you think this language has been confused within policing?
- Why is it important to ensure that everyone understands each role?

Mentoring

Mentoring is seen as a helping strategy for individuals on a one-to-one basis with the aim to aid professional or personal development (Gardiner, 2003). The origins of the word from Greek mythology helpfully describe its role. In the story of Odysseus a father entrusts his friend, Mentor, to take care of and educate his son by asking him: *'Tell him all that you know'* (Bayley et al, 2004). Mentoring therefore is about taking someone on and helping them grow in whatever areas are appropriate.

In a policing context, mentoring is about working with an individual and educating them to assist with their professional development, such as when you take on a newly starting staff member and help them become competent in their new role.

What does a mentoring relationship look like?

Mentoring involves individuals being joined up with protégés for a relatively brief period of time with the aim to promote personal development (Goldner, 2008). Kay and Hinds (2015) describe the relationship well by stating that it is a move away from a managerial relationship to one that is about *'one person helping another achieve something that is important to them'* (p 16), much like the 'In context' example where two individuals work alongside each other. The literature around mentoring positions it as a friendly approach with both parties invested in the development and success of the protégé. This is in contrast to the old-fashioned supervisory relationship we used to see in policing where the trainer often dictated the next steps, sometimes with little explanation as to why, and the student diligently completed the tasks due to the fear of being shouted at.

IN CONTEXT

Police Staff Investigator Sharma is training to become a PIP2 investigator having completed their detective training and achieved a pass in the National Investigators' Exam (NIE). DC Wells has been asked to mentor them and begins with a learning and development review followed by sitting in on a suspect interview. Having completed that, DC Wells discusses with Police Staff Investigator Sharma what went well and what could be done differently to ensure they are a competent interviewer. This process is repeated in relation to a number of detective skills such as investigations, surveillance applications and victim

$\rightarrow$

---

interviews. DC Wells also helps Police Staff Investigator Sharma with their conversational skills to make them a stronger investigator. They work together for a number of months with DC Wells offering advice and pointing out areas which could be improved upon until Police Staff Investigator Sharma is signed off as a competent investigator.

Coaching

Coaching is a bit more difficult to define, as the academic definition is in a state of flux with many different approaches described. This has meant that the boundary between coaching and mentoring has become blurred. It is widely accepted, however, that coaching is more focussed on specific skills, whereas mentoring takes a much more holistic approach (Clutterbuck, 2008).

James Flaherty (2005, p 3) describes the relationship best by saying:

> *If we know what we are intending to accomplish, we can correct ourselves as we go along...coaching is more than just being an accountability partner... or a disciplinarian but sometimes includes these two modalities but goes well beyond that.*

What this means is that coaching does not look at the person as a whole but specifically homes in on what they are looking to achieve. If you identify the end goal, a coach seeks only to reach that goal – so coaching is narrower in its scope.

What does a coaching relationship look like?

Coaching is about goals, and typically a coach will separate these goals into achievable tasks. A coach requires credibility, transparency and rapport in order to set and monitor the goals. It is also reported that a clear end point needs to be defined at the start, enabling success and progress to be celebrated (De Haan and Gannon, 2016) and to ensure the coaching relationship does not go on endlessly when its productivity has ended.

IN CONTEXT

PCSO Perez has completed their probation; however, they have had issues with the quality of their paperwork, which means they struggle to get crime records filed. Support staff Flinn from the incident finalisation team is tasked to assist.

They meet and Support staff Flinn discusses the aim of the relationship, that is to get more matters filed within a shorter timeframe. Support staff Flinn then sets expectations and targets for PCSO Perez to achieve, such as ensuring the right outcome code is used. The newly filed occurrences are then regularly reviewed so prompt feedback can be given and goals can be re-assessed.

After a defined period, the paperwork is seen to improve and PCSO Perez is completing the required actions automatically rather than needing regular prompts. The coaching relationship is therefore brought to an end, with PCSO Perez knowing they can speak to Support staff Flinn should they require further support.

A comparison of the two approaches

Table 1.1 highlights some of the key differences between coaching and mentoring, illustrating that the coach is a more authoritative figure whereas the mentor can be seen more as an adviser or critical friend. Both have a place within policing, since coaching is great to address specific problems which may hamper the performance of a team or individual whilst a mentor looks at the person as a whole, which may be more

Table 1.1 A comparison of coaching and mentoring, adapted from Harvard Business School (2004, p 79)

	Coaching	Mentoring
Goals	To correct behaviour, improve performance and impart skills	To support and guide personal growth
Initiative used	Learning and instruction is directional	Mentee oversees their learning
Focus	Immediate problems and learning opportunities	Long-term personal career development
Role	Coach is heavy on telling with appropriate feedback	Mentor is a listener, acts as a role model and makes suggestions and connections
Relationship	Coach is the boss	Mentor is not in chain of command of mentee (typically)

useful at the beginning of someone's policing career where they are learning core skills, approaches and mindsets.

Any relationship, however, does not necessarily have to sit firmly within one camp or another; it may evolve or change as careers progress. With a student or new officer a mentoring relationship may be the most appropriate, but as time goes on and they gain in confidence and competence it may mean that they require a more directed approach to target areas in which they are struggling whilst allowing them independence in areas they are good at.

REFLECTIVE PRACTICE 1.2

Look back at when you started your current role.

- Who was your coach or mentor and what role did they take?
- Did their role change over time? If so, identify why this might have happened.
- What were the parts of their practice which signalled to you a mentoring role?
- What were the parts of their practice which signalled to you a coaching role?

Conclusion

This chapter has clarified the key differences between a mentor and a coach. Both have an important role to play in staff development. In the context of policing the key is to use an approach that is relevant to your role and experience, is supported by your force or HEI, and suits the needs of your student/staff member.

SUMMARY OF KEY CONCEPTS

- Mentoring is about helping someone develop broadly and holistically.
- Mentoring focusses on a personal relationship with both parties seen as equals.
- Coaching targets specific areas for development.
- A coaching relationship is more like that of a teacher and a learner.
- Both have a place within policing, but you need to tailor your approach to the needs of your coachee/ mentee.

NEXT STEPS IN PRACTICE

- Identify what kind of relationship you currently have with the students or colleagues with whom you are working.
- What are the present needs of those students or colleagues?
- Do you need to adapt your approach at all, and if so in what ways?

Further reading

Bachkirova, T, Spence, G and Drake, D (2016) *The Sage Handbook of Coaching* (pp 195–217). London: Sage.

If you are interested in reading more about the theory of coaching this is a comprehensive and authoritative title with which to start.

It is accessible and also covers working with emotions, use of feedback and values in coaching.

Kay, D and Hinds, R (2015) *A Practical Guide to Mentoring (5th edn).* London: Robinson.

I discovered this title whilst conducting research for this book and cannot recommend it enough. It really distils the key stages of a mentoring relationship and provides guidance on how to navigate that relationship in an easy-to-follow way.

Chapter 2

WHAT MAKES A GOOD COACH?

LEARNING OBJECTIVES

After reading this chapter you will be able to:

- understand the importance of a good coach;
- know the qualities that make a good coach;
- know how to apply these qualities to your practice.

Introduction

Policing is hard and I am certain you will remember your first mentor or coach who helped you at the start of your career. These coaches and mentors are key to developing new officers and staff and understanding what attributes are needed for coaching in a policing setting, and knowing how to apply those skills will improve both the tutor and the tutee's experience of the process. This process can be hard, but it can also be very rewarding. This chapter aims to help you appreciate how these range of skills will maximise your impact.

It is important at this stage to highlight that coaching attributes such as dominance, sociability and openness are not policing-based. Whilst it is important that you are both confident and competent in the area of policing you are trying to guide in, it is important to focus on developing the personal skills which will allow your students to flourish.

> **REFLECTIVE PRACTICE 2.1**
>
> Remember the time when you first started in policing or a new job and think about your mentor(s).
>
> • What helped you learn more?
> • What was not so helpful for you?
> • Why do you think they exposed you to challenging circumstances?

Qualities of a good coach

Angus McLeod, who devised the STEPPA model of coaching, discussed in the next chapter, described 12 key factors which are useful in both coaching and mentoring practice.

1. Authenticity
2. Respectful
3. Hopeful
4. Trusting
5. Patient
6. Valuing people and their solutions
7. Passionate interest in people
8. Inquisitive
9. Status
10. Creative
11. Open-minded
12. Continually developing mental aptitude (McLeod, 2004a)

As you read this chapter, you will find that most suggestions and research tend to come back to one or more of these factors and you may have identified some of these whilst doing the reflective practice exercise 2.1. As you work your way through this book you will discover that you cannot be an expert in every facet of policing; however, by understanding their impact and importance, you will hopefully put yourself in a position to explore those skills when needed.

The impact of a good coach

Most readers can imagine the impacts of a good coach or tutor but alongside these initial thoughts, a plethora of research has been done in this area.

In a study based in Norway, Hoel (2020) reviewed policing students' experiences of their initial post-academy training period. In some cases, students described being thrown in at the deep end and feeling insecure about being in that position. However, despite this, once they mastered being in charge or leading situations in public, many felt a sense of achievement and it even encouraged further learning. This can only have been achieved with the correct support around them; policing is a daunting task and this exposure, whilst a good opportunity, can make people feel overwhelmed if they are not adequately supported.

In a slightly older study, but possibly more relevant given the more academic involvement in the police learning journey, Karp and Stenmark (2010) noted that often policing students were more likely to listen to their police tutors rather than their academic ones. We have seen in England and Wales the academic transformation of police education and whilst students are given a degree-level education in most cases, this study highlights that a substantial influence in students' initial career development is their in-work mentor. As a mentor, therefore, you make their learning to date move beyond the classroom and contextualise it within the 'real world' whilst ensuring they are safe and competent to do the job at hand.

In the same study, new officers were also seen to quickly adopt work methods and habits from more experienced colleagues. If a student therefore is working with other more experienced colleagues, it is important to notice the not so 'good' practice. Whilst the students may see the immediate benefits, they may also not see any issues with it. Without correcting these innocently gained practices, it could be argued that we are mentoring the police student to struggle from the offset. As such, the impact of a good mentor will be seen throughout the development journey of the officer. London et al (2004) suggest that regular coaching and feedback:

> *Play key roles in determining whether goals will lead to performance...and allow an employee to assess progress towards a goal and make necessary shifts in strategy as appropriate.*
>
> (London et al, 2004, p 333)

Put simply, mentoring does not only get students through their portfolio but it also helps drive good performance, expose students to challenging situations and allows them to make changes when they need to in order to make continued progress.

The mentor scale

Chip Bell, a keen writer in the area of mentoring, has devised a 39-question survey which intends to determine whether an individual has the skills to become a good mentor. Its questions look at three key areas: sociability, dominance and openness (Bates, 2019).

These three areas are understandably key in mentoring and can also be beneficial in your policing practice. The importance to policing is discussed further on, but if you want to read more about how this idea came about and the research behind it, please refer to Bell and Goldsmith's book *Managers as Mentors* (2013). You will see in the discussion that follows that whilst these three characteristics are key, there is no set 'perfect' range – in fact, many of them will need to change with time. Where the survey is helpful, therefore, is knowing where you are now and allowing you to reflect on where you need to be in order to maximise your impact.

Sociability

When mentoring, it is important to be able to build a rapport with individuals and not put up barriers. After all, you expect a tutee to be able to confide in you with their difficulties and equally discuss feedback, therefore your ability to easily converse with individuals is key to this process. Even outside of the tutoring/mentoring sphere this is a good skill to hone whilst dealing with the public; the ability to speak to anyone and become 'friends' helps drive engagement, gather intelligence, support victims, and as such good neighbourhood officers should be natural at this skill.

That said, however, you may need to 'dial down' this area when it comes to taking a step back from your mentee, as by putting up some barriers they will naturally begin to learn how to deal with matters themselves and in effect take those training wheels off.

Dominance

Dominance is an area which you would not necessarily expect to see in a tutor but is a key skill to know about if you are in the role. If you are too dominant it is easy to become overbearing towards your tutee or not allow them to take control and slowly expose themselves to those policing experiences which are all too commonplace. On the other hand, if you are not dominant enough with a tutee you may be reluctant to pick up errors, which if nipped in the bud could improve practice early, or you may allow situations to get out of control, which can sometimes happen with a new and excitable trainee. It is a fine balance to have and as your tutee becomes less dependent on you, it is a characteristic which you may need to flex.

Openness

The final characteristic is openness which is also one of the values the College of Policing expects you to display in line with the range of values within the Competency and Values framework (College of Policing, 2016). This trait, however, is even more important in a tutor. First of all, the tutee is naturally going to be vulnerable at times; I am sure we can all relate to a time in our lives when we have struggled emotionally or found an incident difficult to deal with. Part of being a mentor is helping your student understand that it is normal to feel and experience these things, and this variety is why so many people love policing! Equally, your openness is key to providing feedback, as being a closed book means your students may not understand or realise when they are on the right path. I can recall in my training that one look from my tutor constable spoke volumes, especially in front of members of the public when direct feedback is not always appropriate! Having an open relationship is vital.

IN CONTEXT

DC Burn is coaching their first student officer despite being used to working single-crewed in a rural area. After a few months, the student is not making as much progress as they had hoped. As well as looking at their student and trying to support them in different ways, DC Burn is given feedback from a more experienced coach that they do not think DC Burn is giving the student enough space in jobs to take control.

As a result of this feedback, whilst the student has their protected learning time, DC Burn took a free mentoring survey he found online. It transpired that whilst he excelled at the social element of tutoring and being open, he also scored highly in dominance. This is to be expected having worked alone in a rural area for so long, but when coaching, DC Burn now understands the need to control this dominant trait to allow his student to flourish. DC Burn discusses the result with their experienced colleague who provides a few tips such as stepping back from the front door when attending jobs to force the student to take control or allowing the student to work with other colleagues, so they get the space they need.

Mentoring in other sectors

Policing does not work in isolation and whilst the evidence base within policing on mentoring can be thin, other vocations such as nursing and teaching, which are further ahead in their professionalisation journey, have a much broader base of research in the effects of coaching and mentoring. Whilst no job is akin to policing, I am sure many of us can see the similarities it may share with other vocations and the ways in which the mentoring relationship will naturally share key learning ideas and issues. As such, it would be remiss to discount their evidence base in favour of a solely policing one.

For example, much like in policing with the recent uplift, the volume of students to mentors is a struggle in nursing. One literature review (Jokelainen et al, 2011), a study whereby other research is reviewed for overarching themes, found that culturing the right learning environment for students, such as being aware of the students' needs in their portfolios, having regular one-to-ones and ensuring their first shift is with their mentor, may sound like little changes but can be hugely impactive and have research behind them to show their value in student development. Ironically when it comes to being overwhelmed with students this can often be the first thing to be dropped, but effective onboarding into their new role will give them the confidence to flourish.

A study by Huybrecht et al (2011) looked at perceived characteristics of mentors and the impact they had on the mentorship from the perspective of the mentors themselves. Their survey found that characteristics such as being able to give feedback, experience, positive attitude and having time were important for the relationship to work. Interestingly, at the time of the study mentors reported many similar issues that are being reported today by mentors in policing such as time constraints, paperwork, unrealistic views of students and conflicts between education and work getting in the way of effective learning.

Moving to education, a meta-study (Ehrich et al, 2002), a study which reviews other studies and identifies key themes, noted that the most frequent identified positive for the mentee was support/empathy/counselling and friendship. On a practical level this makes sense, as I am sure you can remember your first day with your team and how intimidating it is, but by having regular contact with one individual you build some sort of relationship within the established team and this takes the pressure off what can be an intimidating experience.

The second benefit mentioned for the mentees was the translation from the classroom to strategies they used in practice. If we reflect on policing, we can appreciate the nature of police training as it is often busy and has competing demands. When you learn 'on the street' you often pick up the softer skills required to flourish in the job and this is replicated in research about the classroom.

REFLECTIVE PRACTICE 2.2

Look back on all the lessons from other sectors as outlined earlier.

- Do you see any of these issues or benefits in your own practice, and if so, which ones?
- When you were learning did you witness some of this practice as a student?
- If so, what do you think could be realistically made different to influence your approach?

What do police students value?

Another key point from Linda Hoel's research (2020) was the ability to have easy conversations; many students noted that they often sat next to their mentor in the car which allowed ongoing evaluation and learning. An example of the latter was discussing a job and creating a checklist before arriving at incidents to help them feel more confident.

In a case study about teaching reflective practice to police students Staller and Koerner (2022), argued that whilst the data is limited, the idea of reflective practice was well received by students. This study focused on bringing this teaching to the classroom; a coach could use reflective practice post-incident by giving the student space and discussion points to see how they felt the incident went and areas where they could improve.

In a different study regarding inclusivity within the Swedish police, an interesting point is made about the students' posting locations. It was reported that the policy at the time was to post minority background students to areas which typically had higher numbers of populations which shared their characteristics. Whilst that proved beneficial for the service regarding translation needs and building rapport with the community, students felt that being seen as a resource was also seen to restrict their legitimacy within the police (Wieslander, 2018). When it comes to your practice, if you are involved in postings consider the potential impact a specific location might have in the long-term development and legitimacy of the student and how having the additional strains of being a specific resource might not aid their development.

Finally, Karp and Stenmark's study (2010) identified that a cultural unwillingness to change created issues. In England and Wales recently the police education system has made a wealth of reforms and the impact of this is yet to be truly measured; however, any progress made in the development of student learning could be undermined and devalued by attitudes from experienced officers. As already discussed, these experienced officers are extremely influential on students and as such, they can sway the attitudes of those newer officers, even if innovative approaches end up proving to be more effective. This can slow progress in the service, which we all strive to improve, and it is a difficult balancing act being a tutor having both your own opinions and supporting students to try something new despite being evidence-based.

IN CONTEXT

PC Gin is on a response team and is reflecting on a series of incidents they went to within the same estate. They were reflecting on the incidents, their response and whether they could do anything to prevent further incidents taking place. As a result, they mentioned trying to improve natural surveillance in the estate by cutting back plants and moving some street furniture. However, a seasoned officer who has worked that area for many years turned to them and said, *'You don't need to worry about that nonsense, just get on the beat.'*

As a result of this PC Gin no longer made suggestions about creative solutions to the problem and they continued with their patrols with some success, but incidents continued.

REFLECTIVE PRACTICE 2.3

Consider now if you were the coach of PC Gin.

- How would you approach this situation?
- What would you do about the suggestion?
- What would you do about the seasoned officer?
- What might the impact be if this is dealt with positively?

Having read this chapter you should now understand some factors which impact on whether a student sees you as a good mentor. Many of these skills come down to one key factor: the ability to have open conversations and creating the right atmosphere for discussion. This chapter has discussed police perspectives from across the world and lessons learnt from other sectors who have undergone similar processes to policing. Using the mentor scale, this chapter has highlighted key areas for you to consider when reviewing your own interaction as a coach. Finally, you can see that students enjoy reflective practice. Take a moment to engage in it yourself as you may find it both interesting and a great development opportunity.

SUMMARY OF KEY CONCEPTS

- Policing coaches really shape officers' careers in the initial stages and officers often listen to experienced colleagues more than their academic tutors.
- The mentor scale is a helpful tool to examine how your attributes influence coaching and looks at three key factors:

1. Sociability

2. Dominance

3. Openness

- Professions, such as nursing and teaching, where coaching is far more commonplace have experienced issues that policing may well do in the future and can shape our practice for us to become more efficient.
- Studies have shown that students love conversation, whether that be through reflective practice, challenging current practices or discussing jobs before they arrive.

NEXT STEPS IN PRACTICE

- Assess yourself against the mentor scale and see where you fit in – are there any adaptions you can make that will suit your student now?
- Encourage conversations pre- and post-deployments, discuss possibilities whilst travelling, test students on their legislation, and then on the way back discuss what went well and what could have been done differently.
- Encourage students to work and talk with other officers – we know that students are more likely to absorb information from experienced colleagues, so if you know an expert in domestic abuse and your student has a case to deal with, send them to the expert for a conversation. This will benefit their practice and build up their work network which will help them in the long term especially when working independently.

Further reading

Bates, B (2019) *Learning Theories Simplified.* London: Sage.

This book was recommended to me when I started helping with police student learning, and whilst more theory-based, it is a great introductory book. It discusses many different learning theories and covers each one in just a few pages and in a non-academic way, making it easy to understand, and it also provides suggestions for further reading.

Hoel, L (2020) Police Students' Experience of Participation and Relationship During In-field Training. *Police Practice and Research*, 576–90.

Hoel produces a really interesting article and by reading it you begin to understand the soft skills and little techniques which impacted enough on the student that they commented upon it. You might also recognise that a lot of your own practice which you do subconsciously actually influences the student's experience.

Chapter 3

COACHING MODELS

LEARNING OBJECTIVES

After reading this chapter you will be able to:

- understand a range of coaching models including:
  o the GROW model;
  o the COACH model;
  o skilled helper;
  o the 7Cs;
  o the STEPPA model.
- understand how these models work in a policing context.

Introduction

Different models of working are not uncommon in policing, and similarly, there are a range of different approaches to coaching and supporting people. Whilst this chapter cannot explore them all in depth, it highlights a select few that you may find suits you and your students' approach to learning and leaves a memorable impact.

As you read through the chapter it is worth noting the similarities between the models. This highlights that whilst you as practitioners might not choose to entirely adopt a singular model in your approach, by ensuring you at least have the common areas in mind, you cannot go horrendously off task.

It may also be the case that whilst a particular model suits you, it may not suit your student or the task you are conducting. Having different approaches in mind will help broaden your approach to learning and might allow you to be more successful with your endeavours.

The GROW model

The GROW model is a solution-focussed method coaching framework comprising four distinct stages. It is described as a way to shape a conversation regarding development; however, in a practical setting the model can be used over a number of one-to-one sessions depending on the success of the way forward originally identified. As it is a conversational model, it requires the coach to capture the coachee's interest in order to succeed (Kamarudin et al, 2020).

The stages are illustrated in Figure 3.1. For further assistance on how to apply them and some helpful questions to use in your coaching conversations, please see Sarah Leach's chapter in *The Coaches' Handbook* (2021).

Figure 3.1 GROW model stages

1) Goal setting ➡ 2) Reality ➡ 3) Option ➡ 4) Way forward

Goal setting

Goal setting is important and it should be done when starting a relationship between the student and yourself. These goals should focus on both the immediate and the long-term aims to ensure that the relationship always has a sense of direction. This may be a difficult conversation to have early on, so the two approaches described here may help. Sometimes these approaches are more effective when you give the student enough time to consider their answers to the questions in advance, rather than them using more brain power and energy under pressure having to think of their answer to what can be a complex question.

Two wheres and two whats

This approach is simple and can be given to the student in advance on a piece of paper split into quarters asking four key questions.

1. Where am I now?
2. Where do I want to be?
3. What is in the way?
4. What can I do?

This approach allows the learner to both know their current limitations, their end goal, their challenges and what work they need to do, and whilst they may have some ideas it is within your gift to provide ideas. Having this information to hand will assist in you when you need to have challenging conversations but also open people up to having early welfare conversations which are often awkward in a first meeting. For some learners, being presented with questions can be more effective than the SWOT method.

SWOT analysis

The most common example of realistic goal setting I have seen in policing is SWOT analysis. This looks at four key areas as illustrated in Figure 3.2.

Figure 3.2 SWOT analysis

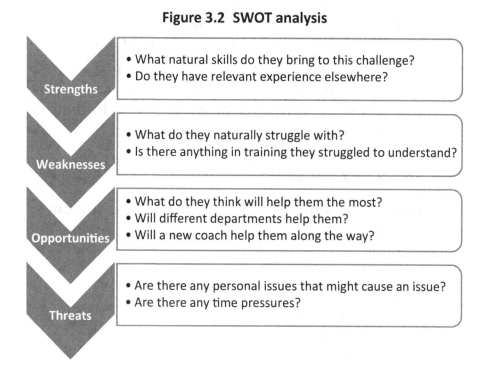

Strengths
- What natural skills do they bring to this challenge?
- Do they have relevant experience elsewhere?

Weaknesses
- What do they naturally struggle with?
- Is there anything in training they struggled to understand?

Opportunities
- What do they think will help them the most?
- Will different departments help them?
- Will a new coach help them along the way?

Threats
- Are there any personal issues that might cause an issue?
- Are there any time pressures?

Again, providing a SWOT analysis to the trainee in advance so your conversation can really explore these key areas is beneficial. You may also be able to allay some concerns or personalise your goals accordingly. Even if there is a portfolio to complete, your intermediate goals could be to address some of their weaknesses, which in the long term will make them better at their role or put them in a better position to learn.

Reality

Reality is about understanding where the learner is now, not only in terms of the goal set but also barriers to success and change and both of the models described earlier will assist with this. The important part is to view the problem objectively. Whilst the trainee might think they know what the issue is, a broader perspective might assist in tackling underlying issues which might provide greater success. If you have been working with a student for some time you might be able to provide an insight that the learner has not yet seen or been told yet. Depending on the goal or task, if it is a broad development goal, 360 feedback might be beneficial.

Option

This stage is about identifying the range of options available to the coachee and not the final option. The key to success in this stage is not only the identification of a range of options but also the exploration as to how they will work in practicality to help identify the next stage. Having this range assists in getting buy-in from the learner when the way forward is selected.

Way forward

The final section is self-explanatory; by having discussed the range of options earlier and knowing their strengths and weaknesses, you should naturally conclude what is the best way forward. What is really important at this stage is an agreement between the two of you, as only with this mutual agreement will you get sufficient buy-in.

Issues with using this model

The GROW model is both simple to understand and simple to apply but that does not mean it is the perfect model. In the context of educating new students, it does not adequately address the depth of development they need. It is much better at resolving singular issues.

In addition, whilst the authors' design was meant to be fluid, the application often means that even if the learner's goal has evolved, as you would expect with competence, the framing at which it is reviewed does not move. This means it does not provide enough stretch or adaption as it otherwise could (Fletcher, 2012). Finally, whilst it is great at deciding a way forward, it does not necessarily review progress, which should be a natural part of your development discussions.

REFLECTIVE PRACTICE 3.1

Remember the last personal development review (PDR) or your job's equivalent which you completed. Using the GROW model, break down one of the goals set.

- Did breaking down your aim help in any way?
- If it did, what in particular helped?
- How could you reflect this in your everyday practice?

The coaching model

The COACH model is similar to the GROW model as it breaks down its methodology into four key stages.

1. **C**larifying needs.
2. **O**bjective setting.

3. **A**ction plan designing.
4. **Ch**ecking activities.

Clarifying needs

Coaching requires a clear set of goals in order to function correctly; however, clarifying needs is much broader than it sounds. The clarification process in its own right provides an opportunity to build a rapport with the learner. This can be done through being professionally curious in the issues at hand and potentially push the boundaries of what the learner thinks might be required (Smith, 2020). Many officers who have done interview training will be aware of 'fine grain detail' required in PEACE interviews of both suspects and witnesses, and a similar level of detail is required here. The better quality earlier on, the more targeted and impactful the approach will be and you will also be much more aware of the support you need to provide to your student.

Objective setting

This reiterates the GROW model with regard to objective setting; however, the SMART(ER) model (discussed later in this book) can also be applied. As discussed in Chapter 1, a key difference in coaching to policing is being to the point and addressing a singular issue, and as a result the advocates for this model push towards trying to improve a measurable factor. They also note that learner buy-in is essential to make this work and if that is not present then it would pay dividends to spend more time on the first part of the model (Champathes, 2006).

Action plan designing

SMART(ER) goals, whilst great for ensuring compliance and progress in the long term, are sometimes not the most ideal when it comes to improving broader areas. Selecting the right action plan design is therefore essential in ensuring good levels of progress. It may be that the defined objectives, such as a portfolio, can be broken down into smaller steps which provide an ideal ground for an action plan, but what is important is that said action plan is both achievable and supported by the trainee. By setting a workable action plan you can sometimes manage what can be a daunting objective into slightly more manageable chunks.

Checking activities

Checking activities in essence is a review of the steps taken against the objectives identified. At this point if the objectives set have not been met, the action plan can be re-assessed and new actions created.

Issues with this model

This model addresses a key issue with the previous model in that it checks back on progress made and allows for adaption. However, it is not perfect, and for this model to work it requires learner buy-in, which, in the initial stages of an individual's career is hopefully not an issue. However, there are occasions in the work environment where individuals do not see the need to be developed and this presents a barrier. In addition, this model requires further building around it. As an example, action plan design is not really discussed, and for some this is a vital element which does not come naturally.

Skilled helper

The skilled helper approach was developed by Gerard Egan and is generally used in counselling or coaching situations where the aim is to achieve lasting change or to empower people to manage their own problems more effectively (University of Glasgow, nd). Whilst it is not a model in the same way the others are in this chapter, it is an approach that you can utilise alongside others to flip development conversations on their head.

The skilled helper aims to use positive psychology to 'help clients identify and develop unused potential and missed opportunities' (Egan, 2002, p 6). As a result, rather than focussing on the issues or the areas for development, he advocates challenging the strengths in order to point out their assets and resources individuals have but do not use effectively (Egan, 2002, p 221). To do this Egan advocates a three-step approach.

1. Allow people to tell their stories.
2. Help them see their blind spots, their problem situations and unexplored opportunities.
3. Help them choose the right problems and opportunities to work on (Counselling Tutor, 2022).

From this approach it is evident that it is likely that whilst the end goal is likely to be similar, if not the same, to other approaches, by taking a slightly different approach, we allow the outcome to be unlocked differently. This model appears to be well adopted within the social work space and as such has a good depth of research behind it, with one study finding that this model is both easily adopted but also allowed those who were being coached to effectively make good decisions without it being imposed upon them (Riggall, 2016). Consequently, it might be a good approach for students with whom it is difficult to have development conversations.

Issues with this approach

This approach is clearly different to the other two and this could be a good alternative to be aware of if you find your traditional approaches do not work. However, this approach focusses heavily on what the learner can see. Whilst the second step wants them to see what 'blind spots' they may have, the reality is sometimes the learners do not see these as an issue. In addition, much like the GROW model it does include regular reviews of any progress.

The 7Cs

The 7Cs of coaching was developed by Grimley and has its basis within neurolinguistic programming (NLP). As a result, it switches the focus of traditional coaching approaches we have seen in this chapter and encourages the coachee to envisage a scenario whereby their goals are achievable (Grimley, 2022). The 7Cs were first established in Grimley's work *Sexy Variables* in 2002; however, the most up-to-date version came from his more recent work in 2019, and he describes the aim of NLP is to:

> *appreciate and work with the coachee's map of the world and co-create new structures in such a way that the experience of the coachee is now more useful in relationship to their goals.*
>
> (Grimley, 2020)

This is an interesting approach if we look at one of the College of Policing's ethical policing principles, respect and empathy. In many of the descriptors it actively encourages us to understand and listen to other perspectives (College of Policing, 2024). If we therefore apply this approach in coaching it makes sense to take on each individual's view of the world and use it to progress them. If policing is to recognise that the diversity in backgrounds adds to the quality of policing it should as a consequence be encouraging our approach to trainees being equally reflective.

The 7Cs are:

- clarity;
- climate;
- capability;
- congruence/confidence;
- commitment;
- communication;
- creativity/courage.

Utilising the 7Cs, as a coach you need to guide your trainee so they understand and appreciate the circumstances needed in order for them to achieve success. Once this is in place they will be able to take action and make positive steps towards their goal, and ongoing work can be used to reflect back on this progress.

Issues with this model

Whilst a different approach, and being receptive to individuals' different views of the world should be advocated, this model for policing might be somewhat too radical. It may be helpful in assisting those that are struggling with other factors and actually need a positive mindset to drive their own decisions, or for those who might not understand how they are ever going to achieve certain goals. The reality of assisting students is that ultimately they need to hit set standards, and the nature of the work may mean that they do not know what or where they need to be to achieve those goals.

The STEPPA model

The STEPPA model, outlined in Figure 3.3, is similar to the 7Cs model but instead focusses on six key areas. Where this model differs is that it is focussed on the concept that emotions play a key role in achieving goals, and consequently by focussing on them we maximise our chances of success (Blackbyrn, 2023). Unlike the 7Cs, this model will be far more suited towards targeting a particular area and as such may not suit those who have a portfolio to do but rather those that have particular issues or skills to address.

Figure 3.3 The STEPPA model

Each step is described in more detail in the next section, other than 'Action' which should be self-explanatory. You should also consider ensuring at some point during the action phase that a review of progress is made; there is no point pursuing an action if it is already not going to plan.

Subject

Subject focusses on the initial conversations with the person you are coaching, answering the key question of 'what do they want from the relationship?'. Equally, the coach needs to establish where that individual is now as there may be personal factors inhibiting progress or it may mean different approaches are needed. In a practical application it is common for an initial one-to-one to take place, and this is where these important conversations need to take place.

Target identification

Target identification has been discussed in other models. However, what is key is to break down the goal into something meaningful and achievable for the mentee. Their initial goal may well be to 'become Super Cop' but that can easily be broken down into small steps such as:

- become confident in doing a safe and legal search;
- become confident in doing a safe and legal arrest.

In reality, any potential portfolio may assist in identifying these goals. But especially in the early stages when these can be quite daunting, it could be valuable to focus the learner on key areas which are either common tasks, such as arresting and interviewing, or goals which you have identified from observation.

By breaking down the goal into targets, the goal is not seen as so unmanageable and too big of a task to take on, and equally progress can be noticed and celebrated.

Emotion

Emotion is a difficult section to manage as unlike the previous two stages it is not a case of simply asking the individual how they feel. It may require the coach to read the individual and confront where necessary. However, understanding the emotions behind the individual can be crucial to making progress, as they can be both an important driver and a blocker to progress.

REFLECTIVE PRACTICE 3.2

Think about your personal experiences either inside or outside of work where: your motivation made it much easier to complete the task; you felt like the task was impossible and did not know what to do.

- Consider how much your emotion halted or improved your progress.
- Looking back on the difficult task, was it as difficult as you imagined?
- Could you have used your emotions to motivate you better?

As you have hopefully seen from the earlier exercise, our brains can easily influence our perception of a task and create mental blocks, and as a coach it is your responsibility to help the student overcome these. I know from personal experience there are times when someone thinks that the task is easier than it actually is, and then dealing with the frustration is another important factor. McLeod, who created this model, describes emotions as both the biggest motivators and de-motivators (McLeod, 2004b) so it is important to understand them early on.

Perception and choice

This section is about getting the coachee to consider what they think their plan of attack is and think about wider options if available. The art here is acting as a sounding board for the coachee to rationalise their best path ahead as this will help get buy-in from them.

Plan and price

Once a selection is made as to the best way forward, creating timelines is important and this will be discussed later in the book when it comes to SMART(ER) goals. Price gets the individual to consider how much personal investment they may require; there is no point making a plan which is doomed from the beginning because it simply will not work alongside either personal or work commitments.

IN CONTEXT

PC Cook wants to achieve promotion and has enlisted the help of a force coach to help them in the process. They sit down together and run through the STEPPA model.

Table 3.1 STEPPA plan

Subject	PC Cook is an officer with five years' experience and has recently achieved a pass in the police promotion exam. Personally, they have just started a family so starting to juggle work and the new dimensions of home life.
Target identification	1. Have enough experience in supervision to become a competent supervisor. 2. Have enough evidence to present in the promotion application. 3. Create a well-written application.

$\rightarrow$

Emotion	During our conversation PC Cook seems well motivated to this task; however, they have mentioned several times their concerns about family life which may be a blocker. Having spoken about their motivations for this, this is a relatively new ambition which may be driven by the financial pressures of having a newborn.
Perception and choice	PC Cook is aware that their current role does not have much opportunity when it comes to supervisory opportunities. As a consequence, PC Cook has three options. 1. Stay in role – accept that opportunities will be limited. 2. Move back to old role – will likely get supervisory opportunities quickly; however, the reason for moving was that they did not enjoy the role. 3. Move to new role – team has been identified, but with no acting supervisor; however, it is a new role and will take some adjustment.
Plan and price	Moving to new role selected, this means that PC Cook can show development in more than one way (laterally and in supervision).

	In regard to the application, PC Cook has some CVF-type examples in mind so will prepare an application so this can be reviewed by a range of people for early feedback.
	Costs – new shift pattern which will need to be discussed with family; however, new station is closer to home.
Action	To be reviewed in six weeks after move has taken place.

As you can see from Table 3.1, in some regards it looks a bit like a decision-making log utilising the NDM model, but unlike policing decisions we have to factor in our emotions as these have an influence when trying to achieve a personal goal.

SUMMARY OF KEY CONCEPTS

There are a range of different models which can be used in coaching.

- The GROW model utilises a number of approaches already commonly seen within policing such as goal setting, establishing options and then picking an approach.
- The 7Cs approach is somewhat different to the other models discussed in that it enables the individual to foresee how their goals will be successful.

- The STEPPA model builds on this, by allowing individuals to target their approach, and rather helpfully it can be built up and written up for work purposes.

NEXT STEPS IN PRACTICE

Each coaching context is different both in regard to the students and the end goal of the relationship so you are unlikely to find a model which suits every scenario. However, the following suggestions should put you in the best place, regardless of the purpose of the relationship.

- Ensure that early in the relationship you understand the end goal.
- Ensure that all goals are reviewed and do not be afraid to say that an approach is not working.
- Feedback is discussed later in this book but it is key to ensuring these models work. Whilst these models provide you with a framework, it still requires the learner to know the expectations and recognise their mistakes.

Further reading

Passmore, S (2021) *The Coaches' Handbook: The Complete Practitioner Guide for Professional Coaches*. Abingdon: Routledge.

If you wish to read in much more detail about a range of models and application in the real world, as well as coaching in general away from policing, I strongly recommend this title. It is highly readable and details both the original works but also its practical application. At the time of writing, for those who have access, it is also available from the College of Policing library.

Smith, J M (2020) Surgeon Coaching: Why and How. *Journal of Pediatric Orthopaedics*, 33–7.

Whilst a slightly unusual source for a policing-based book, I would recommend this article if you are considering setting up a coaching scheme in your particular workplace. The article has a range of well-presented considerations to help try and make your scheme a success. You will, of course, have to disregard the sections regarding medical practices which are slightly less relevant to policing!

Chapter 4

WHAT DOES LEARNING THEORY SAY?

LEARNING OBJECTIVES

After reading this chapter you will be able to:

- understand a range of learning theories including:
  o cognitivism;
  o humanism;
  o group development model;
  o Kolb's cycle of learning;
- and apply these theories in a policing context.

Introduction

In a book about supporting policing students, you may wonder about the relevance of learning theory. Theory is usually backed by research and academic rigor and whilst there will be no one-size-fits-all theory, during your practice you may recognise different theories in action and having done so can tailor your approach to what suits your learner and you.

Theories are often created with a unique perspective in mind; therefore, you may also find elements of each approach in your practice or how your students learn. Given that, there

51

is no need to whole heartedly implement just one theory into your practice. What you could do, however, is cherry-pick different elements to suit you and your learners' style.

Given that this title is work-based, please remember this chapter does not explore the inner depths of each theory, but aims to give you the key points to understand the theories and incorporate them into your practice. If you wish to read more on a particular theory please refer to the references used or the further reading section at the end of the chapter.

Cognitivism

Cognitivism or the cognitivist approach is best explained by the creation of meaningful learning through which learners seek to understand the structure of knowledge. As a result, the focus of the teacher is to help the learner *'learn how to learn'* and *'much of the learning is self-directed'* (Torre et al, 2006).

Jean Piaget was a prominent thinker in this area. He was a Swiss psychologist who was particularly interested in the way thinking develops from birth until young adulthood.

Piaget argued that humans adapt to the environments they are in, and this adaptation is done through two key approaches – assimilation and accommodation. Both of these interact with our schemas, which are best described as building blocks of knowledge, which the brain uses to understand the world we live in (McLeod, 2018).

Assimilation is the process by which new experiences are incorporated within the scope of learning already done.

This means that they make sense of the new event utilising the information that the learners already have.

Accommodation is the concept that existing knowledge is altered to meet the resistance to grasping a new event. In short, when the learner sees something new, they use their existing knowledge and add an additional element to it when it does not quite fit in (Pakpahan and Saragih, 2022).

REAL-LIFE POLICING

You are supporting a student who has just completed their initial training and has no practical application to date of what they have learnt other than watching the true-life police TV shows.

On your first shift you, the student, do two main tasks: the first is arrest someone for shoplifting, which you had done during a practical in initial training and as a result felt confident with the legalities. However, in addition to this, in the real world you got to experience and see how custody process worked beyond what you were told in a presented session and therefore this learning was assimilated.

The second act you did was pass on a death message to a next of kin. You had received no training on this as you were only taught what to do at the scene of a sudden death. Consequently, you accommodated this new learning into your already established knowledge bank (schema) around dealing with death (which is covered later on in this book).

We must look at how we can utilise theory in the real world. By understanding these two types of knowledge processing, as teachers we can consider how best to support and guide our students through their learning. It is always helpful to understand what is included in their training because you can use this knowledge to your advantage and if you present the training knowing what they are exposed to, you can add context in advance.

For a tutor this can be done by reframing the common question *'Did you not learn this in initial training?'* which somewhat undermines the experience given. Instead, you can ask *'Can you remember what they said in initial training?'* This minor change focusses the learner to recall what they were taught previously and show it in their practice, especially if you are able to remind them what was said. In addition, this theory is best applied when learners explore their work, experiment with different approaches, question what is being done and search for answers themselves (Guney and Selda, 2012, p 2335). This would incorporate the knowledge into their practice with much greater depth.

It would be remiss, however, not to mention the potential pitfalls that come with each theory. The most common pitfall with Piaget's approach was the limited research he conducted as all his observations were on his own children! For social science to be tested, it needs to be replicated but using his methodology is difficult as the sample size is both small and he did not provide adequate context for the experiment to be recreated. In addition, for our context of educating mostly adults, the approach being based on children is less than ideal. Piaget also ignored a large chunk of what makes people individuals, such as cultural influences, educational experiences and the influence of peers. It could be argued that this may also impact on learning, but this approach does not adequately explore this area (Babakr et al, 2019, pp 520–1).

Humanism

Humanism is the concept that learners are individuals and naturally search for understanding when they are in the right mindset to do so. As such, when their needs are met, they will naturally be more driven to direct their knowledge accordingly. One paper describes how a student who has low self-efficacy will naturally not attempt difficult projects, thinking 'I am not capable'. Compare this to an individual who will naturally view themselves as dynamic and grow and change (Purswell, 2019, p 359).

Gage and Berliner (1991) established five key principles of the humanistic approach which summarise it well.

1. Students will learn best, what they want and need to know. This means that they need a critical understanding of their current role so they can direct their attention towards the areas they need to develop in.
2. Knowing how to learn is more important than acquiring a lot of knowledge. This element could be argued to be one of the most applicable to policing today; in your own experience how many times has policing practice changed during your service or time teaching it? Knowing how to approach the new practices and adapting accordingly will put learners in the best position going forward.
3. Self-evaluation is the only meaningful evaluation of a student's work. Remembering that this is a humanist approach which is about creating that drive to learn more. However, we must accept that often we work in

an arena of legal constraints and as such for a policing context we must ensure that our evaluations ensure that students are safe and legal. Self-reflection is discussed in other chapters and this is a powerful tool to use to help improve practice.

4. Feelings are as important as facts. From a learning perspective this can be an understandable viewpoint. How many times as a learner have you become frustrated as you are not making the levels of progress you expect when your tutor is happy with what you have done? Negativity can prevent your progress and diminish your drive to learn.

5. Students learn best in a non-threatening environment. Aside from the realities of policing where we will deal with some angry people. It is accepted that an environment where people feel supported over one where they constantly feel under attack fosters a more productive learning space (Huitt, 2009).

In summary, a humanistic approach is therefore quite an optimistic one in which individuals strive for growth within their own personal boundaries, are self-determining, make their own choices and as a result their learning is self-driven (Gould, 2012). For those that follow this theory, learning is best accomplished when the learner's needs are met and then they need to feel safe enough to learn. Finally, self-esteem is important, and they need to feel that every study has equal rights to opportunities (Guney and Selda, 2012, pp 2336–7).

Given this, it is important to ensure that our learners' needs are met, Maslow famously created a hierarchy of needs to ensure that individuals are in the right place. The biggest need is at the bottom of the pyramid.

**Figure 4.1 Maslow's hierarchy of needs,
adapted from Beersdorf (2018) and Cozens (2008)**

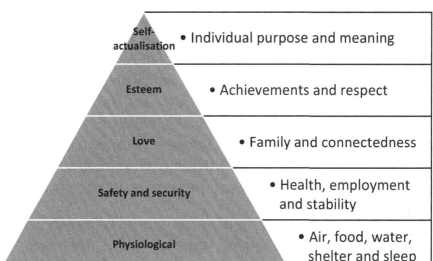

As an individual supporting policing learners, it is important that you support and ensure that where possible these students' needs are met.

REFLECTIVE PRACTICE 4.1

Start from the bottom of the pyramid and consider a time when you have struggled at work or even at home when you have had a task to do because each need is not being met.

- For each situation reflect on whether someone else could have positively influenced that factor to make it less impactful.
- Now consider if you had a tutor/coach/mentor/ lecturer at work, what support would you have wanted them to offer to help mitigate the impact?

Within policing and education providers, a lot of well-being work has been conducted in recent years to help address these different needs, whether that is within each force with different support mechanisms in place, such as mentoring schemes, or through the National Police Wellbeing Service, Oscar Kilo (www.oscarkilo.org.uk/), which provides guidance and support on sleep, mindfulness and health matters, to name a few. Whilst you may not have personally used these services yourselves, it is strongly recommended to be aware of who and what can provide each service so you can effectively signpost should you be required to do so.

Knowing Maslow's hierarchy of needs is important as someone who supports these learners. You may notice, for example, that your student has not had a break or had something to eat especially if we have one of those shifts where everything seems to go wrong and therefore, they do not notice themselves! Part of your role as a role model is to remind the learner or provide them space, even if just for five minutes, to do what they can to meet their needs where possible.

As with all approaches, however, humanism is not perfect. For our context it is hard to argue that new starters will be driven to topics they will need in their role because frankly many often do not know what the role entails. For those that think they do, if this perspective is misplaced then they may put the emphasis on the wrong areas. As this section has also already alluded to, we must also be realistic as to what needs can be met; policing sometimes means long shifts, no breaks and single crewing. Or if you are in a university, you may be conducting lectures on a rest day after a particularly long set. Whilst we need to do our best to support students, we also have to strike a balance with meeting the needs of the public we serve, and different individuals at different times may put a greater emphasis on one need over another.

Group development model

Tuckman created the group development model which looked at both the development of group settings over time and stages of task activity. He argues that both work at the same time; group activity explains the dynamic which operates within the group and task activity shows the behaviours exhibited by the group (Tuckman, 1965).

Group activity

A lot of the development of staff in policing analyses the individual development of a member of staff; however, no one learns in isolation. Whether a PCSO, police staff or officer, it is highly likely that they start their learning in a group setting and consequently for someone who may interact within these settings, this part of the model may be highly relevant for you.

Figure 4.2 Stages of Tuckman's group settings, adapted from Tuckman and Jensen (1977, pp 419–20)

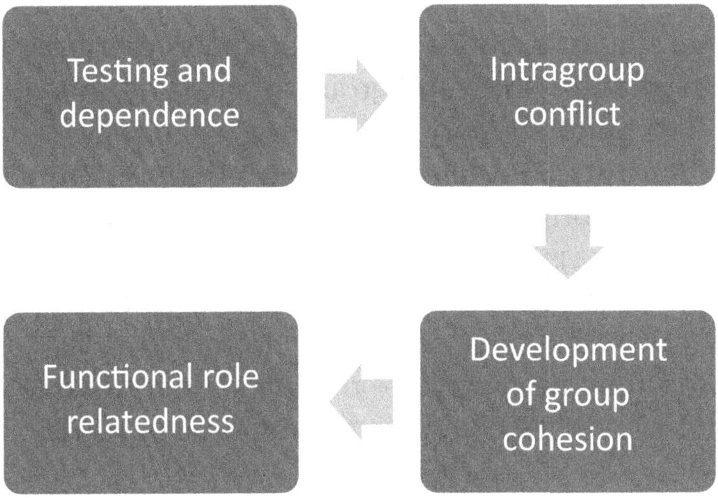

Testing and dependence

Intragroup conflict

Functional role relatedness

Development of group cohesion

The aforementioned four stages can be reduced to 'forming', 'storming', 'norming' and 'performing' (Tuckman and Jensen, 1977, p 420).

The first stage, testing and dependence (norming), relates to the idea that the group become aware and understand the task, create ground rules and test the boundaries for both interpersonal behaviour and task behaviour. If you were ever in a group intake, you might remember when you started you probably did some initial tasks or discussions on what the role involved, the standards of professional behaviour and you may have also done a class contract to establish the boundaries. As a facilitator this is something you can provide structure to.

The second stage, intragroup conflict (storming), is where the group of individuals collide due to wanting to keep their individuality and have yet to fully establish a sense of unity. This can also mean that they may become hostile towards the trainers. Development of group cohesion (norming), the third stage, is the natural conclusion to this phase whereby people start to accept one another, and the roles and norms are settled.

The final stage, functional role relatedness (performing), is the period after which the group as one unit functions to tackle tasks and support one another, naturally therefore people's efforts are then focussed on the task rather than fighting (Bonebright, 2010, p 114; Vaida and Şerban, 2021, pp 92–6). There is mention of a final stage, adjourning, which is the period when naturally all groups come to an end and separate, which in a classroom environment is likely to be the case when they complete training or in a group tutoring scenario when they complete the required portfolio.

Task activity

Figure 4.3 Tuckman's stages of task activity, adapted from Tuckman and Jensen (1977, p 420)

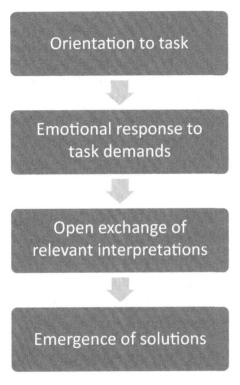

The first stage of the model in Figure 4.3 is about identifying what is required of the group and the method in which they seek to complete it. This includes identifying the information people need to complete the task and figuring out how to obtain it. The second stage is probably one with which many readers can identify, which is having done the first task and then having the emotional reaction to it. This could be in the form of 'I can't do this', or resistance to change depending on the task at hand. The third step is about group harmony. Much like in the group dynamics, this section is about discussing as a group the way forward and ensuring that everyone agrees. The final stage is where we start to see meaningful attempts to complete the task (Tuckman, 1965, pp 386–7).

IN CONTEXT

Singh is a mentor for a new modern-day slavery (MDS) team which consists of a range of policing staff, from uniformed officers, detectives, intelligence officers, safeguarding staff, and those from other organisations such as border force and academics who specialise in this area.

In the initial stages of the group, they are discussing how as a team they wish to approach their task of reducing MDS. Naturally as they are all from different organisations and have distinct roles within those organisations, they intensely debate how it will be done and which organisation will take the lead.

They receive their first investigation and identify the key players, intelligence and available evidence. They then discuss what approaches are available to the team, recognising that each organisation can bring different elements. At this stage they realise that this is a massive investigation and Singh tries to encourage them to narrow their approach to be more effective, but this is resisted, as those on the team argue that they are the ones with the most up-to-date practice.

After a hefty debate, an approach is agreed upon. Rather than targeting low-level operators in this MDS ring, they opt for targeting key players with the intention to stop them operating. To do so they all work together to improve the evidential and intelligence picture, with border force conducting targeted proactive stops, the intelligence officers developing intel and uniformed officers proactively engaging with those they suspect are victims to get them to engage. The detective within the team then engages with the local CPS to ensure the evidential package is suitable for a charging decision when the warrant is executed.

The aforementioned scenario illustrates how the two models can interact in a simple policing example, but this model can be applied to most policing examples. When it comes to supporting students, it is helpful to understand each stage and allow the learners to navigate each stage with the correct level of support. In the preliminary stages, as someone 'in the know', you can help formulate the parameters and information required and in doing so ensure that whatever process goes as smoothly as possible especially in a career when often we cannot afford major mistakes. It is also key to know that you will have to deal with some resistance; this is not because you are doing a bad job but rather because it is an expected normal reaction.

This model, however, is not without issue. First of all, there is a presumption that some groups will go through each stage in order; however, one study (Johnson et al, 2002) showed that tasks that had a short amount of time managed to completely avoid the 'storming' phase. Whilst this model is most applicable in a setting whereby none of the individuals have seniority or have previously interacted, further research will also be required to see whether all the stages are as equally applicable in policing whereby interactions with other officers and teams can be frequent and the rank structure could remove large sections of the debate.

Kolb's cycle of learning

The final theory this chapter discusses is Kolb's cycle of learning, and similarly to the previous model this cycle advocates learning by doing. Traditionally, policing and other elements of the criminal justice system have used experimental learning to ensure that the learning taking place *'is applied in a hands-on meaningful way'* so this should not be a surprising approach (George et al, 2015). Figure 4.4 explains the process. Unlike other theories which prescribe a set order, this model can be entered at any point depending on the type of learner you are trying to support.

Figure 4.4 Kolb's cycle of learning, adapted from Sharlanova (2004)

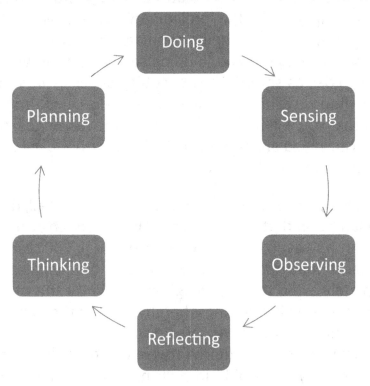

REFLECTIVE PRACTICE 4.2

- Consider your own personal learning style. Based on the previous section, where do you like to enter your learning style?
- Now consider a family member or close friend you may have, where do you think they prefer?
- Is there any reason it is different between the two of you?

Whilst most titles are self-explanatory the valuable elements to this model are the periods of reflection whether that's 'sensing' how it went, or 'reflecting' on an observation and thinking about how to apply it in their own practice. As an individual who supports students, this is where your prompting or guidance can really assist. If you spot an error, rather than being overly critical, it may be more beneficial to craft your questions in such a way that allows the learner to come to this realisation on their own, although on some occasions that is not always possible.

Kolb's cycle fits in well with adult learners. By the time people join policing they would have already established what works best for them and as such there is no need to force them through a prescribed process but rather allow them to develop in a way which suits them.

These benefits, however, are not without criticism. As an example, whilst this model promotes and advocates self-reflection, these reflective impact and learning is therefore limited to what the learner can see (Kelly, 1997). In addition, this model states people can enter the process at a point which suits them; however, in the real world this requires both teachers who can adapt and space to allow this to happen. Sometimes in policing there is a real need to get hands on first and discuss later, and this model simply does not allow for this kind of forced experience.

SUMMARY OF KEY CONCEPTS

This chapter has discussed several different learning theories.

- Cognitivism is about learners incorporating new knowledge into their existing frameworks of information. Piaget argued that it contains two key steps: assimilation and accommodation.
- Humanism argues that people will learn when they are in the right mindset to do so. This means that they need to feel safe in their environment and have their needs met.
- Maslow's hierarchy of needs shows the different *'needs in a sliding scale of importance'*.
- Tuckman created the group development model which had two inter-connected processes running at the same time. One shows the evolution of a working group relationship and the second the approach to tasks.
- Kolb's cycle of learning allows learners to learn at a stage which suits them best, whether that be observing a task or doing it. What it encourages, however, is people to reflect on their experiences and learn from that.

NEXT STEPS IN PRACTICE

This chapter has described a range of learning theories which can be applicable in a variety of different learning environments within policing. To apply this to your practice, however, it would be worth asking yourself the following questions.

- What model best suits the learning environment you are in?
- Are there parts of your practice which already fit in with these or other models?
- Are there parts of the practice which directly clash with the theories discussed?
- Is there anything that you could introduce which would maximise the learning utilising the theories?

Further reading

Gould, J (2012) *Learning Theory and Classroom Practice in the Lifelong Learning*. Exeter: Learning Matters.

This book is a really accesible and affordable title to help those interested in expanding their knowledge in learning theory and its application in the real world. In addition, for those that like to avoid academic language this title strips a lot of that out, and I would recommend this as a good book to add to the collection.

Johnson, S D, Suriya, C, Yoon, S, Berrett, J V and Fleur, J L (2002) Team Development and Group Processes of Virtual Learning Teams. *Computers and Eduction*, 379–93.

Online education is increasingly taking place, so for those that have to facilitate this and encourage group work in such settings, this article is an interesting read, especially if you have an interest in the group development model.

Part 2

Helping student development

Introduction to Part 2

Part 1 has hopefully provided some contextual and some of the more 'academic' side to supporting students. Whilst this can often be overlooked by those in policing, you will find that by understanding some of these approaches and knowing where your personal preferences lie, you will as you go through this next section be able to identify which approaches you will prefer more easily.

This second section of the book relates to the acts of developing the students and does so over four chapters. Whilst the last two chapters work hand in hand, any of them can be dipped into should you need advice.

The first chapter in this section relates to leadership. When it comes to supporting students, some may think this topic an odd selection. However, whatever role in policing you may have involves a level of leadership. The public quite rightly look at police officers, staff and volunteers to take control at an incident, and developing this skill is of importance. What can also be overlooked is your development as a police leader as a result of supporting a student – this is also discussed.

Chapter 6 relates to personalised learning. Many of those within policing may have heard of learning styles; personalised learning is the next evolution of this but is different enough to require a change in working practices.

That is not to say, however, that the old learning styles will not be of use to your practice, so this is also discussed.

Chapter 7 moves onto the more everyday work you will do whilst supporting students by discussing conducting reviews and setting goals. This chapter features the commonly used SMARTER model and mentions Gibbs' reflective cycle. This skill should be core to supporting students, as without them knowing the direction of travel and their progress against this, their progression may be slower than anticipated or slower than what the student could actually achieve.

The last chapter in this section relates to giving feedback. As much as some learners may hope, no one is perfect at everything on their first attempt and that includes those providing the feedback! This chapter discusses the importance of giving feedback, some considerations you should have prior to giving the feedback, before finishing with some different models of giving feedback you could consider in your practice.

I hope this section is of use. For those 'do-ers' this section is intentionally aimed at you and whilst all of the contents will not necessarily be new to everyone, at least some of it should challenge your current practice or give you some new ideas going forward.

Chapter 5

LEADERSHIP

LEARNING OBJECTIVES

After reading this chapter you will be able to:

- understand the need for student officers to display leadership skills;
- be able to foster leadership skills with those that you support;
- understand how coaching can develop your own leadership skills.

Introduction

Leadership in policing is essential and goes beyond traditional rank structures and is the responsibility of every member of staff. Whenever the public interact with policing, they expect control and direction in any situation and as such expect leadership skills (Rogers, 2008, p 5). The public do not know if it is an officer's first day after initial training or if they are coming to the end of their 30-year career, therefore fostering these skills is essential in your role in supporting policing students.

Supporting students, however, is not just about their leadership skills. If you are in service, supporting students will also benefit you and it is only right that this is acknowledged so that is also discussed in this chapter.

The need for leadership

The police have and always will be role models to the public. If we look at the Peelian Principles, there is a great emphasis on securing public favour and ultimately allowing policing by consent to happen (GOV.UK, 2012). Without appropriate leadership, even back when these principles were written, this is simply not possible.

The College of Policing in its Leadership Review (2015, p 6) highlighted four dimensions to leadership.

1. Individual
2. Operational
3. Senior
4. Organisational

It can be argued that supporting students need to focus on the first two dimensions. The College state that everyone needs individual leadership to flourish in their role and that operational leadership is key for incident management and team effectiveness, both of which are key for those roles which are public facing. Regardless of what role a student might be training for, both skills will be tested and evolve throughout the initial stages of their career, and this development will continue throughout their career within policing. Whilst the focus should be on the first two dimensions in the initial stages, that is not to diminish the importance of the latter two which are needed to ensure all staff are both supported and allowed to develop.

It is also important at this stage to highlight that the culture of policing has, in recent years, been under immense scrutiny. In Baroness Casey's report into the culture of the Met she stated that *'predatory and unacceptable behaviour has been allowed to flourish'* and that the Met in particular *'does not easily accept criticism nor "own" its failures'* and that *'the culture of not speaking up has become so ingrained that when senior officers seek candid views, there is a reluctance to speak up'* (Casey, 2023, pp 12–13). Whilst some may argue that this report focusses on only one in more than 40 forces in England and Wales, it is still one which is seen as the key player in policing and, if we are being realistic, it will not be the only one with such attitudes. It is also worth adding that the report emphasised that the vast majority of officers act with the best of intentions. Yet this is just one of a number of reports which highlights the importance of getting leadership right from the bottom to the top.

Leadership now, more than ever, is key to policing and as those guiding new staff through their developmental period it is vital that you instil the best in them and aid their development where needed.

REFLECTIVE PRACTICE 5.1

- Can you remember a time when in the early stages of your career you were shown a level of control in a situation?
- At that point in your career did you feel ready?
- Were there any skills or experiences you had that helped you deal with that scenario?
- Is there anything you wish you had known?

What is expected from an officer?

Upon completion of the reflective practice exercise, you may have realised that when you first started in policing, you may not have recognised policing as a demonstration of leadership. Alternatively, you may have even looked back on that situation and realised how far you have come since starting your career!

For those just starting it is hard to know what is expected of you, especially when your perception of the role may be based on recruitment information and TV shows! Clearly, in training, legalities and assessments go some way to helping those understand the core of their role; however, the 'soft skills' are often unexplained but are arguably the most impactive.

The College of Policing (2023a) recently announced leadership standards, which are staged depending on an individual's role within the organisation. Understandably this section will focus on stage one, leadership foundations.

Leadership foundations highlights 15 key areas that staff and officers are expected to display. None of these should be either a shock or are overly revolutionary, and are about:

- acting ethically and doing the right thing;
- serving the public;
- managing yourself in both performance and well-being.

As someone who supports students it is your responsibility to ensure that your students act in accordance with the aforementioned areas as you play a key role in making abstract learning such as being told about the Code of Ethics (College of Policing, 2023b) translate into real-life behaviour.

IN CONTEXT

PC Alyse has just started their uniform patrol period of their initial training. During their academic elements of learning they were taught about how ethics became more prominent in policing and in their police training they were told about the Code of Ethics.

PC Alyse witnessed some unprofessional behaviour in the office and did not know what to do as they were new on shift and did not wish to rock the boat.

Consequently, they went to their tutor to ask for advice. Their tutor explained why it was so important that this behaviour was tackled and apologised to them for having witnessed it.

PC Alyse's tutor then directly addressed the behaviour with the colleagues as this was the most appropriate approach given the circumstances.

This circumstance helps illustrate that to an extent whilst we can tell students about the importance of leadership and ethical behaviour, our actions speak louder than words, and as a role model this should be expected of you.

Developing leadership

Anyone can be a leader; however, like most skills in life, some people are better at it than others. Whilst personal qualities are without doubt important, behaviours and skills can change and can be developed with practice (Boon, 2015, p 10).

A tutor or coach quite possibly has the hardest role in developing leadership as they must apply classroom learning to the real world when most of the content previously taught is still somewhat abstract. This has to be done at the same time as working and ensuring the needs of the public are met. This section does not intend to repeat the contents of previous chapters; however, it will highlight some techniques you could use to help people develop. It is worth highlighting that these do not have to be used in isolation and can be tailored to the needs of your student.

Modelling

This technique, in my experience, is very popular with students and as such it is introduced with some reservation. In certain situations, it is hard for a new student to know and understand what the job requires of them. This may be because they have not been exposed to it, they may not have grasped the previous learning, they struggle to apply concepts to the real world or they lack the confidence to have a go. In these circumstances it can be of value for a tutor to model what they expect, but remember that on occasions if confidence is an issue sometimes actually doing the task will help overcome this much more effectively. Within policing, modelling is often taken literally where a tutor will take control of a scenario to show the trainee. However, modelling can be a much lighter touch. In an earlier chapter, this book discussed the value of students being able to have conversations with the tutor in the police car on their way to an incident, and modelling can be used in this scenario in the pre-arrival discussion. This way the learner can still be exposed to the situation but will understand what is expected of them and have a recent example to work from.

Providing opportunities

When I was young in service, I often just wanted to concentrate on getting better at the role I was doing and as such often shied away from opportunities. Within policing, however, there is a concept known as 'volun-told'. This is where, whilst those who need the task doing would happily take a volunteer, your supervisor instructs you to do it as it would be a great 'developmental' opportunity.

It is important to ensure that those you are supporting are exposed to the right opportunities for them to be both productive in their role and develop their leadership skills. Sometimes there is a pressure to push students towards opportunities they are not ready for, which from personal experience can often put their progress back. Equally, however, a healthy change can really help push progress at times. Part of your role, considering you know the students better than potentially anyone else, is to guide those around you as to what opportunities would be best placed at that particular stage of an individual's development.

Debriefing

Within policing, debriefing is sometimes seen as a meeting you would only do following attendance at a major or critical incident. But within a tutoring relationship it can be as simple as a five-minute conversation in the car. Whilst supporting a student there will come a time when you cannot continue to keep modelling and need to let them experience the tasks for themselves. Debriefing tries to ensure that the impact of such an experience is consolidated and is the most impactful, highlighting both what went well and what needs improvement. It is important during the early stages of an individual's career that when discussing incidents you do not just focus on the legalities of their actions but rather encourage constructive reflection on their control and interaction whilst dealing with the matter at hand – in the long term this will make them more effective.

REFLECTIVE PRACTICE 5.2

- Early in your service do you remember an incident where you did something legitimate in your practice but for some reason it did not land well, or the situation unravelled quickly?
- Following that situation what learning from it was discussed?
- On reflection do you think there were any previous incidents where a little bit of advice might have helped you handle the situation differently?

Discussions

The final approach is one we often see in job interview circumstances to see how others work in a team or to try and elicit candidate's thoughts and opinions on a topic. But within a group environment such as in response teams this can be a good approach to discuss topical matters in policing. As this chapter has already discussed, policing has not been without controversy in the last few years and equally policing is not without staff who have an opinion! So why not use this to develop people?

A recent example of this could be the increasing prominence in policing regard VAWG, Violence against Women and Girls. As an example, following the case of David Carrick, a former officer who was described as a *'serial rapist and violent sexual predator'* (Kelly et al, 2023), it transpired that there were several opportunities to potentially intervene within policing. This provides a natural talking point and allows an experienced supervisor or someone who leads a group of students to discuss the what-ifs, were they to encounter such behaviour. Discussing and knowing the next steps might empower an individual who is unsure of what they should do to act.

Leadership for you

Whilst it is important to ensure we establish great leadership skills in new officers from the start, it is also worth highlighting the benefits supporting a trainee officer can bring to you and how it can help your ambition to take on a greater leadership role should you want to. For some, taking on such a role is their first unofficial foray into line management, and whilst there is plenty of development to be had there are also plenty of opportunities to maximise success in your own endeavours.

Most importantly when it comes to applications, we have to consider the Competency and Values Framework from the College of Policing (2016) which should play a key role in most application processes. It is quite easy to argue that whilst supporting policing students you are exposing yourself to a range of scenarios which will provide very easy examples in a board. Consider having to work alongside academic tutors, student support officers and the student themselves if they are not hitting the mark and require intervention as an example of collaborative working. Or supporting a student through a difficult period or challenging incident and ensuring their and your needs are met as an example of being emotionally aware.

On a more practical level if we look at the book *Blackstone's Leadership for Sergeants and Inspectors* (Boon, 2015), you will see echoes of what it describes as core skills for these ranks whilst you are supporting students such as:

- delegation;
- problem solving;
- motivation;
- interpersonal skills;
- giving feedback – which is also discussed in Chapter 8;
- meeting skills.

What is key therefore is ensuring that you maximise these opportunities for both yourself and the person you are supporting. This way not only will they benefit from your insight, but you will also benefit from the challenge they provide you. It is worth noting that with any development journey learning leadership skills is not going to be a simple upward trajectory. At various points mistakes will be made; however, as is the case in most policing situations, owning them and learning from them is a valuable asset it its own right and can make great examples of personal reflection. I strongly recommend keeping a record of some examples as you come across them, as it is quite easy to forget your good work. A few lines about the situation might be an ideal prompt when it comes to writing applications.

SUMMARY OF KEY CONCEPTS

In this chapter, we have discussed leadership for both the learner and those supporting them.

- It is clear that leadership in policing is important in all roles, not just when it comes to dealing with the public but also internally, and it ensures that the high standards the public rightly expects are maintained.
- When it comes to those you are supporting it is likely that they will be in a role the College of Policing expects to show 'Leadership foundations'. Whilst these comprise 15 standards they can be shortened to three key themes:
  1. acting ethically and doing the right thing;
  2. serving the public;
  3. managing yourself in both performance and well-being.
- Developing leadership can be difficult; however, there are a range of ways you can demonstrate it to those that you support, whether through modelling, providing opportunity, debriefing or facilitating the healthy discussions sometimes required.
- Looking after policing students is also beneficial to your own development goals. Many key skills needed to effectively manage people are tested and developed whilst supporting others, and for those who may need evidence for promotion aspirations taking on such roles maximises opportunities you may not have otherwise had.

NEXT STEPS IN PRACTICE

- Do you know your own leadership development areas?
- Identify opportunities where you can help those you support grow.
- Have the confidence to have difficult conversations, whether that be in a debrief following an incident or discussing a policing topic currently in the media.

Further reading

Boon, B (2015) *Blackstone's Leadership for Sergeants and Inspectors.* Oxford: Oxford University Press.

For those starting their promotional journey, I would personally recommend this title and I have seen those who I would consider to be good leaders refer to this title. Much like the next title, it focusses on the key skills needed to perform well. Most importantly it tackles each area in a minimal amount of pages, meaning if you urgently need advice, you can find it quickly.

Rogers, C (2008) *Leadership Skills in Policing.* Oxford: Oxford University Press.

This book, whilst a slightly older title, is a great read if you want to expand your leadership skills. It covers key areas including motivating staff, meetings, leading operations and leading during times of change. Most importantly it does so in an easy-to-read format, with little to no academic speak, making the title highly readable.

Chapter 6

PERSONALISED LEARNING

LEARNING OBJECTIVES

After reading this chapter you will be able to:

- understand what personalised learning is;
- understand the difference between personalised learning and learning styles;
- know how to apply this information in your own practice.

Introduction

Whilst learning in a police setting I have always been aware of people's different learning styles. As someone who supports students you should be mindful of these and adapt your approach accordingly to help suit them. Personalised learning is a newer approach and is about making this process commonplace and less about having to act 'differently' for a particular individual but rather make different approaches normal and commonplace. Whilst this may sound difficult there are some new approaches which can be used to make this easier, and this chapter helps explain these.

Personalised learning goes beyond different learning approaches and aims to tailor the training time to the needs of the learner. That said, however, that is not to say that your previous knowledge of learning styles is no longer of use; as an individual supporting students you can combine the two to make your practice more efficient. This chapter does not intend to make you overhaul your practice but rather encourage you to reflect on your approach and see if personalised learning is something that you can adopt.

What is personalised learning?

Personalised learning is an educational approach which rather than repeating the same lessons to different cohorts of students much like a 'cookie cutter', it advocates customising the learning to each student's strengths, needs, skills and interests (Morin, nd). The US department of Education describes personalised learning as:

> *instruction in which the pace of learning and the instructional approach are optimized for the needs of each learner. Learning objectives, instructional approaches and instructional content all may vary based on learner needs.*
>
> (US Department of Education, 2017, p 1)

This description does not suggest that this approach encourages you to rip up your potential approach to the PEQF curiciculm and start again. But rather tailor our approach to the different learners' needs.

The ultimate aim of personalised learning is to address the disengagement researchers have seen in today's students and close up achievement gaps (Hughey, 2020). In a policing context this can only be seen as a good thing as by addressing learning barriers, we potentially allow for a more diverse workforce and less attrition within the existing pathways.

REFLECTIVE PRACTICE 6.1

Consider a time you were learning something in a classroom and just did not understand the content.

- Were you given enough opportunity to understand the content?
- If so, what did the trainer do to assist with that?
- If not, is there anything the trainer could have done?
- When/if you learnt the content did you find your approach was different to others?

Within a policing context how can this be achieved?

The application of personalised learning sounds daunting. Feldstein and Hill (2016) suggest that this can be done in three ways.

1. Flipping – traditionally class time is spent 'broadcasting information' such as in a lecture. A personalised method of this is flipping what you would do in the traditional classroom time. It is argued that broadcasting information can be done outside of the classroom such as on an e-learning portal. This means that the contact time you have can be used to have conversations where individuals' weaknesses and strengths can be fully explored.
2. Turning homework into contact time – in a traditional set-up, educators typically do not see a lot of the work the students do. As an example, homework is a task where often those who struggle with something are hidden away from those in the best place to support them. Even the outcome of the work only provides limited insight as it does not provide the context of the struggle or the time it has taken. By utilising the 'flipping' approach,

these activities which explore and expand understanding can be done in a more supportive environment where approaches can be tailored to each person.

3. Provide tutoring – this does not have to be in a way that is time- and resource-intensive. An example given in the article is adaptive learning software which personalises the learning journey, gives feedback and provides the information to the educator so they can use it to influence their work.

What is interesting about the aforementioned approaches is that it should not require an extra investment of our time, merely a change in our approach to the use of our time. When considering policing education some of these ideas may not be directly applicable in all areas but there are elements which can be used. For example, the concept of flipping can be easily introduced for those sessions whereby there is not much debate or sensitivity in the topics being taught. This would then allow the educator time to spend on one-to-one tutorials or additional practice for the students. Homework, however, is more troublesome and I would like to hope that this is somewhat minimal especially in police initial training, as students need time to recover and reflect, and being a workplace, they should not be expected to learn for free after hours! Helpfully much of the skills practice, such as arresting, is seen in person during training, so feedback and assessments can be conducted in the moment. Finally, tutoring is commonplace especially during the stages of initial training. However, other opportunities can be maximised, especially online learning which is traditionally formulaic and lacks personalisation. However, should the broadcasting of information be introduced where this learning will inevitably shift online, this allows for the creation of such content.

A note at this point should be made regarding personalised learning implementation. Given that it requires a rather large upheaval in teaching approach and allocation of staff time it is not something that can be trialled in one classroom. It is likely to need a complete timetable re-design, considering staff availability, how mastery is recorded and assessed and flexibility in teaching approaches depending on the needs (Rawson et al, 2016). Realistically in policing this could be done by targeting some sessions which are broadcast heavy in order to give the space to trail the implementation of 'flipping'.

However, policing is not one for completely scrapping what has always been done and therefore if you are looking to implement, this may be a good starting point. As an example, personal safety training could be an interesting area to look at, especially the learning provided in the initial stages of someone's career. Within initial training, we see important messages being sent out in the broadcast sessions, but do these sessions really need to be in person if they are showing a video or utilising the same presentation? The discussions, however, and the skills can be delivered in a personalised way, even in groups if needed.

IN CONTEXT

Police staff Borne is learning how to create e-learning content as part of their role. Traditionally this course is done with an input showing how the software works, followed by a workbook that candidates do in their own time which is assessed to show compliance.

$\rightarrow$

There was a trial of a new format prior to their attendance. Police staff Borne completed an interactive e-learning that provided them with an understanding of how the system worked. Having done this, police staff Borne was provided with the opportunity to create the content they needed to using protected time. As progress was being made, the trainer reviewed the creation, in the time usually allocated to the class, and sat down with the learner to discuss how it was going and offer some potential tips.

Police staff Borne preferred this approach as they struggle to pay attention in long periods in the classroom especially when the content is particularly dry. However, they benefitted from having one-to-one support in the areas which they did not realise needed improvement.

What are the benefits to this approach?

The key benefit to personalised learning is that it encourages a smarter use of time; if one input is always going to be the same, why enforce that part to be in person? Whereas the elements where you test and expand knowledge, or where there is a practical element to it, might be better suited to this time. The reality is we currently live in an era of personalisation, whereby the growth of mobile technologies and many other organisations have created an ecosystem that allows for personalisation, and as a result consumers often need on-demand personalised content and experiences (Groff, 2017). Given this, it makes sense to meet the needs of the future generations we intend to educate by doing the same within policing.

As already mentioned, the intention is to help aid education and be more responsive to the needs of the students. If this is successful, then some of the attrition we have been seeing in the initial stages of police development (Police Federation, 2022) might be addressed. However, it would be naïve to argue that attrition is solely due to the police education, and this area is a much more complex discussion suited elsewhere. If you are interested in this topic the works of Sarah Charman and Jemma Tyson (2024) are a great read.

What are the risks and issues of this approach?

The reality within policing is that the organisation requires set standards from our officers and staff to help maintain a minimum level of public service. When an officer, for example, hits the frontline, we expect a baseline of knowledge to ensure they can operate both safely and legally. Full implementation of this approach requires a robust and effective benchmarking system to ensure that minimum standards are met. Given that much practical observation during initial training is done whilst being taught, this will need to be reviewed to ensure that it continues to meet the standards required.

Many roles in policing also tend to be recruited in bulk, such as call handlers, PCSOs and officers. Given the bulk recruitment, some of these intakes can be sizeable, and this was especially the case during uplift when targets were set. If we were to use the concept of 'flipping' with intakes of this size, how much time realistically will each student receive? In addition, there is also the risk that those that make the most noise will get the most help, which will not always address inequality. Having access to the results of the remote learning and using that to tailor staff time is vital to making personalised learning work, and are we confident that the level of feedback educators will receive is of sufficient quality and detail to allow them to be as impactful as needed?

Finally this approach seemingly puts a great deal of weight on e-learning, which within policing has been shown to be not as effective as we would hope. In a study one member of staff was quoted as saying, '*I find it very boring, it's not productive at all, cos I just switch off*' (Hardy et al, 2020, pp 10–11). This led to a sentiment that e-learning lacked engagement and interaction, meaning those being trained were not invested in completing them and then consequently had low pass rates and reports of cheating through sharing answers. This may be because of the way e-learning is typically deployed within policing, to deliver key messages quickly. But for personalised learning to succeed, investment will be needed in this area and there needs to be a better plan for delivery. That said, however, there are a range of academic institutions that have engaged in e-learning and successfully taught degree level topics exclusively online. With the greater engagement with academia the PEQF has brought this may be a successful area for development and as an example the Open University already teach using the PEQF.

Learning styles

Prior to individualised learning the more popular approach in policing was learning styles and these approaches were split into three key types:

1. Instructional preferences – relating to students' desired learning environments.

2. Information process – includes attitudes about their own academic programming.
3. Cognitive personality style – works on classic theories of information processing (Antoniuk, 2019, p 85).

Personalised learning naturally leans towards individuals' cognitive personality styles and instructional preferences. These areas have been around for some time and whilst a particular methodology is in vogue the research learning from these studies can be equally beneficial.

Cognitive personality styles

Honey and Mumford are two of the more popular writers when it comes to this and referred to these styles as learning styles. Their work was originally aimed at managers within the workplace and they devised a survey to help indicate which style individuals leant towards. This survey resulted in one of four approaches to learning (see Figure 6.1). You may notice that these four types are similar to some of the stages discussed in Kolb's cycle of learning (Cassidy, 2004, p 432), which is discussed in Chapter 4.

Being aimed at managers, the survey is particularly helpful when we discuss police education, as the previous chapter discussed to varying extents, we expect all those in policing to be leaders and as such should not be seen as the ultimate barrier to using it.

It is also important to highlight that these styles are not intended to be an ultimate guide to how people learn but the survey is seen as a method to getting individuals to give some consideration to how they learn and to tailor their approach accordingly (Coffield et al, 2004, p 74).

Figure 6.1 Learning styles and their characteristics, adapted from Bates (2019, p 124) and Rosewell (2005)

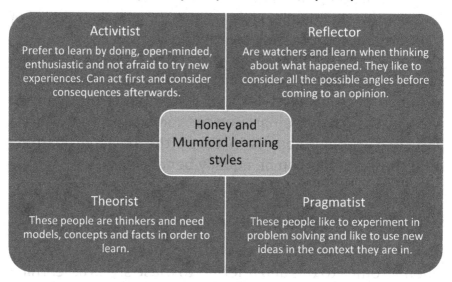

These learning styles are not mutually exclusive. In one study it was found that 35 per cent of individuals have one strong preference, 24 per cent had two strong preferences and a further 20 per cent had three (Coffield et al, 2004, p 73). As a consequence, when it comes to tailoring our practice and helping people learn, the best approach is to provide a wealth of different methods which would appeal to each type rather than putting all your educational eggs in one basket.

One interesting paper utilised these learning styles and found that different methods of presentation on e-learning suited different styles. For example, reflectors watching a video input had a correlation value of .796 (the closer to 1 the better), which showed it was highly effective, whereas a simulation tasks with those with the activist trait had a correlation of .85 conversely; however, those activists reviewing the same the video had only .131, meaning there was little connection (Sangvigit, Mungsing, and Theeraroungchaisri, 2012, p 1316).

This approach is clearly a great start when it comes to adult learning, and the survey devised may assist you in tailoring your approach to students. However, it is clearly not perfect. As previously mentioned, only 35 per cent of people had one particular preference, and some papers have argued that some of these approaches are so similar that it would be better to narrow them down to two or three where you combine both reflector and theorist as many of the skills and traits are shared (Leung and Weng, 2007).

Information processing

Information processing is seen more commonly within policing, and you may know it as 'VAK learning styles'. VAK stands for:

- **V**isual;
- **A**uditory;
- **K**inaesthetic.

Each style summarises a different way in which an individual may process and store information.

Visual

Visual learners typically learn better when using their eyesight to learn. As a consequence, pictures, demonstrations, notes and mind maps are likely to be useful to them. It is worth noting that some research separates verbal and non-verbal visual learners. Those that are verbal lean more towards text content whereas those non-verbal prefer more pictorial content.

Examples of ways to incorporate it into current practice could include:

- colour coding material;
- highlighting prominent areas of text;
- drawing concepts;
- using maps and images;
- doing activities that employ visual skills such as word searches and word matching activities.

Auditory

Auditory learners prefer to hear content and as such find content containing video clips, taking part in discussions and being able to listen to lectures particularly helpful. They can retain information better when it is presented in a rhyme or song.

A few examples of incorporating this into practice could include:

- allowing them to learn somewhere they can listen to the content;
- group discussions;
- having content to audio stream;
- encouraging activities such as brainstorming and sharing of stories.

Kinaesthetic

Finally, kinaesthetic learners prefer to learn through feeling and experimentation. As such they like to have physical experiences and as such are not suited to virtual models of learning (Kanninen, 2008, pp 15–16). Unlike the other two approaches this approach is much harder to incorporate into a normal style input, but ways of putting this into practice are:

- role-plays;
- field trips;
- focusses on practical work rather than theory (Hussain, 2017, pp 33–6).

Why have we moved away from learning styles?

The reality of tailoring our instructions and educational approaches to these styles is that it demands considerable time and resources to do so. This would be fine if it was evidence-based, which all policing practice should be slowly working its way towards; however, there is a lack of research to support these approaches (Pence and Snyder, 2017, p 1). In one example of research the researcher looked at whether different types of learning style preference equated to more aptitude in a particular area and the study found no statistically significant link at all (Rogowsky et al, 2015). In addition, most research into learning samples by the very nature of research has a restricted sample size which is often limited by the location of those who volunteer for the research. This then means that any generalisations are unique to that area (Antoniuk, 2019, p 87).

Finally, when it comes to more scientific study of the VAK learning styles there are very few pieces of research which make it to legitimate journals (Cuevas, 2015, p 328). As a result in an era when policing is trying to make their work more evidence-based it seems bizarre to embrace a practice which is far from being evidence-based.

How can I apply all of this whilst supporting a student?

This chapter has introduced personalised learning, which for those in traditional education settings would be easier to implement. However, as someone who might be on the front line, time is precious and it would depend on the content you are trying to relay. If it were legislation or policy you could direct your students to resources which would give them the key information, meaning the personalised element could help you reinforce that information.

Whilst learning styles have been somewhat debunked, individuals' preferences are still important. After all, the approach is personalised, so if an individual prefers a certain VAK presentation of information there is usually a range of different sources available. Also, if a learner does not know what they prefer, the quiz might provide some insight into what works for them especially if as a reflector they need time and space to think.

IN CONTEXT

CSI Lynch is learning about forensic recovery and is struggling with a certain element of it. Their tutor is struggling to present it in a way which works and asks how they would prefer it done. CSI Lynch explains that they are one of those people who likes to read about it in a book (visual) and then think about how it would work in a real-world scenario (theorist/pragmatist). Their tutor saved a CPD session where this method was explained and allowed them to take it home to read and digest.

Having done this, the tutor discusses with CSI Lynch how it is going to work and checks their knowledge.

CSI Lynch shows an improved knowledge but wants one element shown to them, as having read the book they cannot see how it would translate in real life.

Rather than show them, the tutor opts to get CSI Lynch to give it a go with them by their side. They explain the principles and work through it together.

This example is just one case study, but we must also remember that we cannot in a time-critical role always accommodate each type of learner. As someone who supports students, it is your job to understand what works for them and adapt where you can. But we have to accept in policing that this is not always possible. If, however, your role provides you an opportunity to plan, keeping in mind various different types when creating sessions will help appeal to as many people as possible. If you are going to use 'flipping' we also have to be practical. If much of the information is going to be provided ahead of a session can we realistically expect them to have time to read or listen to the content? If not, then how can we factor that time in?

REFLECTIVE PRACTICE 6.2

Using the aforementioned typologies, have a think about how you best learn and absorb information.

- How can teaching styles be adapted to suit both your types?
- Now think about someone who is the opposite to you. How could someone engage both you and them in one session?

SUMMARY OF KEY CONCEPTS

In this chapter we have discussed the following.

- Personalised learning is a way to tailor the education we provide to meet the needs of the learner.
- Personalised learning can be achieved in three key approaches:
  o flipping – taking the broadcasting of information out of the classroom;
  o turning homework into contact time;
  o personalised tutoring.
- Cognitive learning styles have three distinct types, two of which were the focus of this chapter:
  o cognitive personality styles – Honey and Mumford produced the survey which allowed them to find a main style which works for them;
  o information processing – much research in this area focusses on the VAK approach:
    - visual;
    - auditory;
    - kinaesthetic.
- Despite the latter styles, however, there has been little empirical research into it and those that have taken place do not necessarily add weight to the argument that these approaches are valuable in aiding learning.

NEXT STEPS IN PRACTICE

- Do you know how your students prefer to receive information?
- Do your sessions focus on the understanding of information rather than the reception of it?
- Do you still put too much emphasis on learning styles?

Further reading

Cassidy, S (2004) Learning Styles: An Overview of Theories, Models and Measures. *Educational Psychology*, 419–44.

If you require a really punchy description of different types of learning styles, some of which are not discussed in this chapter, this is an excellent article to read. It describes each approach in a few lines, describes how the approach is measured and also mentions key concerns and where such a model has been supported so you can have an early indication of whether it suits your potential use.

Coffield, F, Moseley, D, Hall, E and Ecclestone, K (2004) *Learning Styles and Pedagogy in Post-16 Learning: A Systematic and Critical Review.* London: Learning and Skills Research Centre.

This particular paper is quite lengthy; however, it not only describes the learning style approaches in great detail but it also explains how its utilisation in the learning, pedagogy, is influenced. Given that this also looks at post-16 education, the step to adult learning is much smaller when we come to many other papers looking that look at theory.

Chapter 7

CONDUCTING REVIEWS AND SETTING GOALS

LEARNING OBJECTIVES

After reading this chapter you will be able to:

- understand best practice when it comes to conducting reviews;
- know and understand:
  o the SMARTER model;
  o Gibbs' reflective cycle;
  o the role and use of 360 feedback.

Introduction

Whilst supporting students it is vital that we review their performance and set goals. Doing so in a way which is a positive experience for all can be beneficial for both the students learning and your management of them. This chapter aims to provide you with different approaches to make the process of reviewing and setting action plans easier. This chapter also works hand in hand with the next chapter which is about providing feedback.

Reviewing performance

Reviewing an individual's performance can be tricky and often in practice it is not done as often as it should. It is especially difficult in policing as it is a people-based role and as such 'good' might look differently to others. Add to this complexity the challenge when we already know someone's performance is not quite up to scratch! That said, however, reviewing someone's performance should be commonplace especially in the initial stages of a student's development, and often forces have established frameworks to ensure that it is done.

Reviewing an individual's performance is a difficult space to work in. In policing we work in a subjective space with very little objective variables and as such this can create a feeling of unfairness, whether that be procedural in that those being reviewed do not believe in the process or the outcome where individuals object to how it has made them feel (Winstanley and Stuart-Smith, 1996, p 68). As a consequence, having an approach which hopefully addresses both needs will go a long way.

The first thing to establish is what is the point of a performance review? A singular review cannot include every single element of working in policing. Therefore, if we cannot be clear about the aim this can often lead to directionless discussions which become a tick-box exercise rather than anything meaningful. The Policing Vision for 2025 states that:

> *the service provided is critically reliant on the quality of its people...the service needs to create a culture that values difference and diversity and which*

empowers individuals to maximise their contribution through continuous professional development and the encouragement of reflection and innovation.

(National Police Chief's Council and Association of Police and Crime Commissioners, 2016, p 8)

A number of reports which followed this highlighted the need for policing to have a learning culture (Brierley, 2022, p 238), and reviewing an individual's performance easily works towards this goal. An article in the *Harvard Business Review* states the reviewing performance is to:

- allow an accurate and actionable evaluation of performance;
- allows individuals to identify areas of feedback so they can improve on their skills (Cesoedes, 2022).

One such way of allowing an actionable evaluation is to discuss areas of work in line with Gibbs' reflective cycle.

Gibbs' reflective cycle

When it comes to reflective practice, Gibbs' model is one of the most commonly cited, and as discussed later is often seen used in other parts of the public sector. Gibbs' reflective cycle can be used in a number of ways, such as using it as the basis for a reflective conversation, a written piece, or some universities promote it as a basis for their essays! Whichever approach you use, knowing this model might allow individuals to be able to review their performance and this self-reflection can often be more powerful than individuals having it told to them.

Figure 7.1 Gibbs' reflective cycle, adapted from Potter (2015)

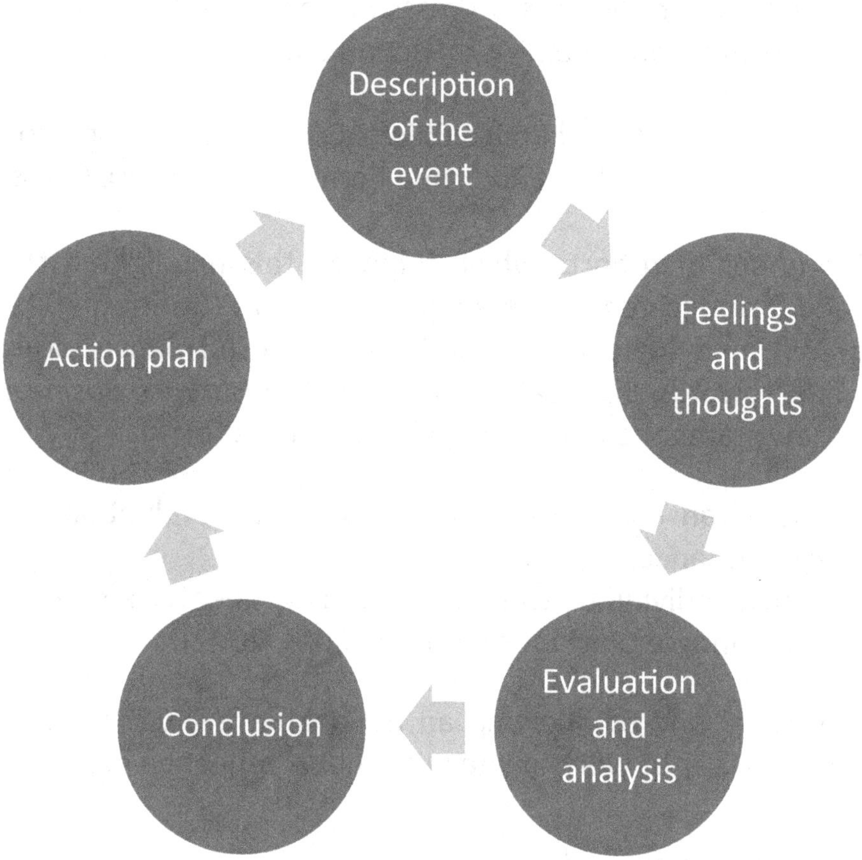

Description of the event

This stage is a logical place to start when it comes to looking back on one's own performance. This is not so much about the why but what took place, and getting a good level of detail here means that the following stages can be hung onto various events which have already been described.

Feelings and thoughts

Feelings and thoughts are much broader than what the person reflecting was thinking there and then. It can sometimes be quite powerful to get them to consider how they feel looking back on the incident or even how they consider other people were feeling about the situation (The University of Edinburgh, 2020). By considering other viewpoints, the individual reviewing their own performance broadens their viewpoint.

Evaluation and analysis

This section is self-explanatory but having discussed the earlier points, it is now worth discussing what went well and how performance can be improved. The most crucial element here is the why; this helps the learner understand processes and policies and also means that this learning can be translated to other situations. Even if a particular incident was catastrophic there will always be a positive to pull from it, and having that balance is important.

Conclusion

Gibbs in this section proposed two forms of conclusion.

1. A general conclusion – focussed on the transferable knowledge.
2. Specific conclusion – focussed on the situation.

These are now often merged but the concepts are important to remember. You need the learner, having reviewed their performance, to look back at the incident and know where things were both good and bad but also know what they need to work on and what they need to maintain (University of Cumbria, 2020).

Action plan

Setting goals is discussed shortly, therefore there will not be much focus on this other than to highlight its importance. When reviewing performance, sometimes people see the reflective element as the difficult part, but its real impact is when you decide what to do with it next.

Issues to be aware of

Gibbs' model is widely used, especially within nursing. One paper studying the nursing use of the model (Timmins et al, 2013) raised concerns that often those supporting individuals were not effectively guiding their students through the model and as such it lent itself to superficial use, rather than a meaningful tool. As a result of this, when using it in policing whether in written or verbal, make sure that this is done with vigour and detail and does not become a tick-box exercise which people do not engage in.

The same paper also found that many people do not want to share their reflection with a stranger and found the process jarring especially when asking about their feelings on random topics. One example given was how children use IT! This highlights two key issues. First, for someone supporting policing students it adds great value to already have some sort of relationship with the learner; if you do you are far more likely to get better results from this model. Second, when discussing emotions, it must be done so with purpose and the questions tailored accordingly; when it comes to policing, most situations have an element of human impact, even if implementing a new IT system.

Table 7.1 Warrant reflective cycle

Section	Comments
Description	6 am warrants conducted at five addresses across the county. Briefing took place at 5 am for deployment at 5:30 am. Two warrants ended up taking place at 6:10 am due to travelling distances, one child was put into police protection as a result of the attendance. Large quantity of drugs has been recovered and suspect interviews completed, main players in the organisation have been remanded following superintendent extension and others are now on bail. All warrant conducting officers were released on time.

$\rightarrow$

Table 7.1 (Continued)

Section	Comments
Feelings and thoughts	Initial thoughts are that the warrant went well, since that time I am frustrated that not all happened at the planned time and that evidence could have been lost if they were alerted. In addition, the charging process was stressful as we were pressed for time.
	Hopefully, the suspects are frustrated with our disruption efforts, but I am concerned about the well-being of the child, who we were unaware of prior to attendance, the method of entry caused particular distress with the PPE worn.
Evaluation and analysis	These warrants were successful and key evidence has been obtained which was of vital importance to the investigation. The late execution of two warrants is easily remedied by allowing a longer amount of travelling time and getting the various units to have a rendezvous point nearer to the location in case of traffic etc, and best-case scenario just means we simultaneously execute the warrants earlier than planned.
	The superintendent's extension was unplanned and this was in part due to the length of time for phone data to be recovered. It would have assisted CPS greatly if we had early engagement with them prior to the warrants so that they could have fully reviewed the evidence rather than being pressed for time.

Section	Comments
Conclusion	Generally – allowing greater time in the schedule for contingencies will help improve the smooth running and take pressure off staff, and greater engagement with partners such as social services and CPS may help the day run better. Specifically – warrants were executed well, drugs and evidence recovered and a child effectively safeguarded. Traffic is difficult to account for, but this has been learnt as has early engagement with the CPS.
Action plan	See the action plan section.

From Table 7.1 you can see how the operation of both reviewing performance and setting goals can and should work hand in hand. As someone supporting students it is your responsibility to ensure that not only do they know what went well and what could be improved, but also to ensure they do something with that information!

360 feedback

Another common methodology to assess performance is using 360 feedback. This is a process in which subordinates, peers and bosses provide anonymous feedback. This is done alongside one's own assessment of themselves to see how they compare, which has shown to be most beneficial especially if an individual rates themselves higher than those rating them in the anonymous survey (Brett and Atwater, 2001, p 930).

The College of Policing have their own 360 feedback tool which specifically focusses on police competency and values.

The College of Policing argue that using the tool:

- allows for individually tailored and focussed development;
- improves self-awareness;
- provides specific feedback on individual skills, abilities and behaviours;
- identifies areas of strength and development;
- assists in constructing SMARTER goals (College of Policing, nd).

That is not to say, however, that even within policing the College of Policing tool must be used. For example, it can be run by an individual independent of both the recipient and the sample. Or it can be done utilising commonly found software such as Microsoft Forms. For it to work, however, you need to ensure that anonymity is assured to those giving the feedback, including where possible to include more than one person from each category (supervisor, subordinate and peers) to ensure that their identity cannot be figured out based on the nature and content. Also, by getting multiple feedback adds greater depth and makes it more reliable.

360 feedback is not, however, without criticism. When it comes to reviewing performance in particular we need to be careful as to what the 360 feedback is measuring. Often it measures behaviours and attitudes rather than the typical metrics on which you would conduct a performance review (Beehr et al, 2001, p 784). Both of these, whilst important, have key distinctions which users should be aware of. When we are looking at policing students, therefore, just because a 360 feedback session highlights areas of development

does not mean that they are not able to do the role safely and lawfully.

In one study, which reviewed its implementation within the Patent Office, it found that the person receiving feedback had the onus on acting on it on themselves and this next step was not perceived to be part of the process (Morgan et al, 2005, p 674). The next part of this chapter discusses setting goals, which will prevent such issues from occurring. But as already discussed, reviewing performance is only worth doing if next steps are considered.

REAL-LIFE POLICING

You are new to the role as acting sergeant. Having been on the team a number of months, you know that you are not the finished product yet. You are particularly worried about the soft skills required to lead a team effectively. When you ask those you lead for feedback they simply respond with *'you're doing a good job, don't worry about it'* or words to that effect. You did not find this helpful and it left you somewhat directionless regarding areas to develop.

Alongside your professional development team, you decide to utilise 360 feedback, asking your current sub-ordinates, sergeants you work alongside, and your management for feedback. Whilst you do not know who responded, it appears the team are frustrated with certain members who are seemingly getting away with doing less, whilst others feel they are not adequately informed about what is going on in the force. Interestingly, a few superiors noticed that despite handing down messages for you to relay to officers they do not feel they have been acted upon. This made you realise that communication between yourself and the team is a key priority. To address this, you adjust the way you brief at the beginning of each shift, you have also started to monitor workloads closely and challenge those you feel are not doing their fair share.

Setting goals

Now you have reviewed performance and potentially identified areas of both praise and improvement the next step is to set goals. This is your space as someone supporting students to ensure that they set goals aiming for something which is both meaningful and worthwhile. One common trend I have noticed is there is sometimes a fear within policing to set action plans. This is possibly due to their use in the unsatisfactory performance framework which could lead to an individual's dismissal. However, if we look at what their core role is, it is far from being a stick to beat people with but rather a way to ensure that people are held to account and make steps towards their goals. They ensure that if an individual is not quite hitting the mark this is checked up on and then if further support is needed it can be put in place rather than leaving an individual to flounder and sometimes suffer in silence. Consequently, if action plans or goals are used with the correct intention, they are fair and supportive. There should be no fear to use them within the service.

REFLECTIVE PRACTICE 7.1

Think about a time you were set a goal whilst at work.

- Were you happy that it was imposed upon you? Did you think it was fair?
- Did you understand fully why it was given to you?
- Did you think it was achievable?

The SMARTER approach

One common method both in and out of policing for setting goals is to use the SMARTER mnemonic (Chartered Management Institute, 2011). SMARTER goals can be used widely within development conversations to really push performance and interest in an individual's own goals. In Lawlor's study they found that students often procrastinated in a given task, and the use of this approach they hypothesised helped push towards earlier completion (Lawlor and Hornyak, 2012).

SMARTER stands for:

- **S**pecific;
- **M**easurable;
- **A**chievable;
- **R**ealistic;
- **T**imely (or time-bound);
- **E**valuate;
- **R**e-adjust.

In practice, you may find both slightly different wording and sometimes just the use of the word SMART. None of these word changes make a hugely significant impact on the use of the mnemonic, and each letter still represents something within the same spirit, therefore one preference over one word or another should not be criticised. What is important is the use of the last two letters 'ER', as without these, goals can often be left unchecked and unadjusted. It should be widely expected that an individual's development is not a linear journey and therefore why should their goals expect them to be?

The next part of this chapter discusses what each heading means before giving an example which shows it in action.

Specific

It is quite easy when it comes to reviewing a performance to just say *'you're rubbish at paperwork'* but very rarely is it the entirety of a task that an individual needs a goal for. Often when comments are made about paperwork it can be refined with details such as *'you need to improve the detail in your case files regarding the points to prove'* or *'you need to improve your spelling and grammar'*. This level of information is important when setting goals with students as by keeping it broad they may not actually know what needs to be looked at. Also, when it comes to reviewing the progress with a broad goal, it is quite easy to criticise another issue that the learner may not have been aware of, which in the eyes of the learner would be unfair.

Measurable

Having a measurable goal means that when it comes to the latter stages you will be able to know whether there is noticeable improvement. When developing individuals, we do not expect them to go from zero to hero in the space of one action plan. So even if their performance is not perfect you can still acknowledge the progress that has been made.

Chamberlin (2011, p 25) used the word 'trackable' in their work and this can also be important as they argued that being able to easily see ongoing progress towards the final goal helps those working towards the task as they do not want to wait until six months is up before they can check how they did.

Achievable

This element seems quite self-explanatory: there is no point setting a goal no one can achieve, for to do so is demoralising and for a student in their development likely to be quite damaging. When it comes to police performance as an organisation, we can afford to strive for more in our ambitions but in this context, we are not seeking gold standard. My partner who is a teacher uses the phrase '*good is good enough*' and I think this is a fair way to express this element.

Realistic

We cannot expect an individual within two hours to singlehandedly solve a murder, remand the individual and produce the casefile to CPS. So why when it comes to development goals should we expect anything unrealistic? This element is like being achievable, but also considers the timing of the goal and where the student currently is.

Timely (or time-bound)

Firstly, you would not want a goal which was relevant to your development three years ago. It is unlikely to be relevant and if you were subject to it, this would be extremely frustrating. Timeliness of goal setting is therefore important during the initial stages of someone's career. So, if a development plan is utilised sometime after the goal is set, it is highly likely to be irrelevant.

The time-bound element relates to the individual knowing when they are expected to show progress by. This is to make sure that progress does not flounder and that they are kept accountable.

Evaluate

When it comes to goal setting, goals are designed to be something which we expect an individual to reach, therefore it makes sense to see what progress is being made. This is not to say that every initial goal will be met and achieved; however, the successes and shortfalls should be recognised. Given this, it is imperative that evaluation is not a black and white pass or fail but understands and acknowledges the shades of grey in-between.

Readjust

This stage follows on naturally from the previous stage. As already mentioned, not all goals can be met with 100 per cent success. Knowing what we do from the evaluation phase, the question we need to ask now is: *'Do we need to adjust the aims and objectives to better suit the learner and ensure effective learning going forward?'*

Prior to moving on it is worth highlighting that there are several slight variances online as to what SMARTER stands for and how it is applied (Brown et al, 2016, p 3). As such, whilst this chapter outlines the author's suggested approach, if your force/service uses a slightly different alternative, the bulk of it will be the same and the content and suggestions are equally as applicable.

IN CONTEXT

Let's return to DC Jury's action plan. As already mentioned, it is likely that this investigation is going to require additional multiple address warrants. So, this action plan was designed to ensure that improvements are seen in the next sets. Whilst the plan detailed in Table 7.2 is brief, depending on your development goals, it can be expanded accordingly.

Table 7.2 Warrant SMARTER plan

Specific	Ensure that warrants are executed correctly and at the same time to prevent loss of evidence.
	Have early contact with the CPS for them to review the evidential picture to make in-custody charging more efficient.
Measurable	This can be measured through the operation of the additional warrants and seeing how they work and reviewing the evidential product to ensure that all evidence received is lawful.
Achievable	Yes – the first round of warrants went well and some minor learning from last time will improve the process.
Realistic	Yes – most of this can be done in advance of the day of warrants, not putting DC Jury under additional pressure.

$\longrightarrow$

Table 7.2 (Continued)

Timely	This is direct feedback from the previous operation and is therefore very timely especially as no warrants have been executed in between times. Most of these improvements need to be made before the next phase of warrants to limit any further loss of evidence and should not delay them.
	This can be reviewed after the next set of warrants, the timing of which is long enough to allow sufficient progress to be made.
Evaluation	Review of CPS contact can be done in the weeks leading up to the warrants.
	Timings regarding the execution of warrants can be done on the day or in the post debrief.
Readjust	Depending on the advice from CPS, there may be a need to readjust our evidential package to assist them in reaching a charging decision.
	Depending on how the timings go for the next warrants, there is likely to be more than one phase of warrants and as such we can review and adjust timings accordingly.

SUMMARY OF KEY CONCEPTS

In this chapter we have discussed the following.

- Gibbs' reflective cycle which consists of five key steps.
  1. Description of the event.
  2. Thoughts and feelings.
  3. Evaluation and analysis.
  4. Conclusion.
  5. Action plan.
- 360 feedback is another method of conducting reviews whereby anonymous feedback is gathered from subordinates, peers and managers.
- The use of SMARTER goals and how the use of them is important to ensure feedback is not ignored but rather acted upon.
- That evaluation and readjust are key stages to this process, development is not a linear process and as such neither should our goals be.

NEXT STEPS IN PRACTICE

- Do you know how your force records action/ development plans?
- Have you reviewed previous action plans you have set to ensure they adhere to best practice?
- Have you utilised any of these tools on your own performance?

Further reading

Chartered Management Institute. www.managers.org.uk.

Another great website if you are looking at different management skills is from the Chartered Management Institute. Some of their content requires you to become a member, which you can either pay for or obtain through doing working towards one of their qualifications; however, it is a great source of CPD and has a library of knowledge to draw down on which is both evidence-based and practical. I have personally completed one of their qualifications and would recommend it, but you would benefit from having space and time to engage with their range of services.

The University of Edinburgh (2022) Available at: www.ed.ac.uk/reflection (accessed 16 January 2025).

Whilst researching for this title, I found this amazing resource from The University of Edinburgh. It provides a wealth of resource to individuals either hoping to reflect on their own performance or for those who wish to facilitate reflection.

Chapter 8

GIVING FEEDBACK

LEARNING OBJECTIVES

After reading this chapter you will be able to:

- describe the importance of good feedback;
- understand some key considerations when providing feedback;
- be aware of different approaches to feedback including:
  o the seven steps to feedback;
  o stop, start, continue feedback;
  o starfish feedback;
  o AID feedback.

Introduction

Feedback throughout your career is vital; it is the only way you will know what went well and what could be improved on. But the art of giving feedback is also just as important; delivering feedback in a way which, despite well intentioned, lands poorly can do more harm than good. This chapter briefly discusses the importance of feedback before explaining key considerations and different approaches to giving feedback.

The importance of good feedback

When people hear the phrase 'good feedback' the mind often goes to being told what went well. Good feedback refers to the quality of its delivery including how the content is presented. Policing is a person-based service and rightly everyone involved comes from a multitude of different backgrounds. This is great but also means that universally we will not all have the same strengths and weaknesses. Therefore, without the ability to give effective feedback these areas which we naturally struggle with will never improve.

Boon described feedback in a policing setting:

> *commenting in a constructive, assertive way on the behaviours and performance.... identifying and remarking on good progress and difficulties and tackling any obstacles to the completion of tasks and objectives. Importantly, giving feedback opens a dialogue with those receiving it.*
>
> (Boon, 2015, p 120)

These are quite clearly key skills when supporting an individual in their student phase. For some, however, feedback can be awkward to approach and there is a fear of getting it wrong. To those people, however, I would ask them to reflect on the cost of not providing feedback when it is needed. Davenport (2022, p 104), who discusses challenging conversations, suggests the following, among others, as consequences of perhaps not having these conversations:

- tolerating poor performance, and individuals thinking their behaviour is acceptable;

- behaviour influencing others' views on what is acceptable;
- tension within a team, especially if others have to work harder to compensate;
- reduced effectiveness or productivity;
- deprivation of an opportunity to improve.

Whether you are a supervisor, tutor or have some other involvement in policing, these are clearly impacts you do not wish to experience. Whilst these are understandably generic when it comes to the impact of giving feedback and having challenging conversations there is also a wealth of research which supports the idea of giving feedback.

Johnson (2012) found in their study that fostering supervisor feedback and informing them about what is expected of them in relation to performance fostered an officer's sense of organisational commitment. At a time in policing when we are continuing to strive for more performance, have extended shifts to deal with public order situations as well as other factors, spending a short time providing good effective feedback can make difficult decisions, which will impact upon staff finish times, well-being etc, a little bit better received.

Considerations for feedback

In an article which focussed on peer feedback, Dahl et al (2023, pp 229–31) suggested six factors that impacted upon the reception, uptake and impact of feedback.

1. Timing.
2. Content form and mode.
3. Frequency.
4. Relationship.

5. Specificity and level of support.
6. Individual traits.

Most of these factors are self-explanatory regarding how they can impact on the effectiveness of feedback and should be considered prior to giving feedback. Even if in your opinion you feel like feedback needs to be immediate, consider whether someone might need space and time to reflect on what happened, referring to the previous chapters. The in context feature later on provides an example when a combination of these factors can make the feedback less than ideal.

Timing

Timing is important in most things – executing a warrant too late can be disastrous, being too slow to respond to an incident can be fatal – but timing is also important when it comes to feedback. Chapter 10, which deals with death, discusses well-being support plans, and it is important to consider similar factors when providing feedback. Just imagine being late off a night shift and your supervisor pulls you into the office to provide some feedback that could really wait, especially if you are already frustrated with what happened.

Drago-Severson and Blum-DeStefano (2017) listed in their title, *Tell Me So I Can Hear You: A Developmental Approach to Feedback for Educators*, some key factors which would influence the decision to wait when it comes to feedback:

- time and space are needed for independent reflection;
- emotions are running too high (for you or others);
- waiting would not be unduly risky for individual or organisational well-being;

- delaying feedback feels like a developmental support;
- the moment is not right (others present, no space, participant is busy or the relationship is not right at the time).

There will always be times when immediate feedback is needed, but being aware of the aforementioned factors will make you consider timing more effectively and therefore make your feedback more impactful when you get it right.

Content form and mode

Form and mode relate to how the feedback is presented, whether that be orally, written or in another form. Interestingly there is no consensus on what works best. Some studies have found that the written form is preferred by candidates whereas others have found that verbal is preferred (Dahl et al, 2023, p 231). From personal experience, getting someone to read anything typed is important, as text can often be interpreted in many different ways.

Whichever way feedback is provided, there is some advice on some of the approaches you could use later on in the chapter. From a policing perspective, it is strongly recommended that whatever form the feedback is provided, it is recorded. Whether that be in a learning and development review or via email, even if the recording is after the feedback has been given, which means that should the feedback process have to enter a more formalised process you can already evidence what has been said. It also saves the 'you never told me that' argument which can happen when learners switch off when being told something they may not want to hear.

Frequency

Frequency is important. Imagine working in policing and being in the same role for five years but it's only in the fourth year that you are provided with feedback that says you are not performing well. This would be both frustrating and confusing as in the years leading up to this, surely there was an opportunity to provide you with at least some feedback.

Frustratingly this is not uncommon in policing. In one study that looked at police interviewing only one quarter of respondents stated they received feedback on their work. This is despite other research showing that lack of feedback can lead to a dramatic decline in skills (Snook et al, 2012).

Consider this when you are in a position to provide feedback, do not just save your moments for when something bad has happened. Little and regular feedback makes the conversations more commonplace and less awkward when you need to have challenging conversations.

Relationships

Relationships is an interesting topic. This can best be explained in Kim Scott's opening pages of *Radical Candor* (2018). Scott argues that people who trust you and believe you care about them are more likely to:

- accept and act on your praise and criticism;
- tell you what they really think about what you are doing well and not doing well in;
- engage in the same behaviour with one another;
- embrace their role in a team;
- focus on getting results.

Clearly these traits would greatly impact on the uptake and impact of feedback and shows the value of having the right relationship to give effective feedback. In policing there will be occasions where others will need to give feedback but as someone supporting students sometimes your role will mean taking on others' feedback and using your relationship to deliver it with impact.

Specificity and level of support

As discussed in the previous chapter regarding SMARTER action plans, being specific is key. It is far too easy to be too broad with your feedback and then the true crux of the issue be lost in translation. By being specific and offering the correct level of support, you maximise the opportunity to see results from your feedback. It is also important to note that the level of support for two people experiencing the same issue could be entirely different. Support cannot be a one-size-fits-all approach, with large numbers it is sometimes easier and logistically manageable to provide the same all round. If that is the case, however, be wary that some elements of support will land better than others with different sections of cohorts.

Individual traits

A lot has been written about individual traits and responsiveness to feedback as it is a well-researched area in psychology. For example, one study found that asymmetric feedback, where there is either a weighting towards positive or negative feedback, differs to balanced feedback, where there is an equal amount of both. When the feedback focusses on areas of improvement, it is much better received by those who are high and confident performers, whereas it found such feedback for low performances to be detrimental, suggesting it was not worth them participating in the feedback (Buser et al, 2016).

Another factor to consider is your own personal traits, as often within policing 'feedback' is given without enough time to reflect and potentially calm down! Unless safety-critical, more often than not feedback can wait, as long as it does not become irrelevant due to an excessive delay. In my experience, people who want to give feedback hastily often do so for the wrong reasons.

IN CONTEXT

PC Whitlock was working alongside DC Adair during their probationary CID attachment and they had been working together for the last five weeks. As there was a detained person they wished to remand, naturally the shift overran.

Whilst sending the case to the Crown Prosecution Service (CPS), DC Adair realised that the material had been added to the casefile incorrectly, meaning it all had to be downloaded and re-uploaded again, adding significantly to their lateness. Both of them finished at around 3 am rather than the scheduled 6 pm.

Having finished the shift, DC Adair wished to provide feedback to PC Whitlock so they could learn from their experience. DC Adair decided whilst it was fresh in his memory to compose an email on his work device, hoping that PC Whitlock would read it at the beginning of their next shift.

At the same time, however, PC Whitlock was typing an email to DC Adair, thanking them for the interesting shift and how they enjoyed working on a case which was working towards a remand. Having sent the email, they saw the feedback.

Being overly tired caused PC Whitlock to get upset as they were hoping to sit down with DC Adair in the next shift and discuss how the case went, as they were aware they had made a mistake but also thought there was a lot that had gone well. PC Whitlock formed the opinion that DC Adair was just looking for the negative and did not focus on what went well and they have never been thanked or praised for helping on the DC's other cases.

Also, on review of the email, whilst aware that something had gone wrong, PC Whitlock did not understand where or how it was their fault, as being told to *'learn the basic functions of the system'* was neither supportive or helpful.

REFLECTIVE PRACTICE 8.1

Consider the aforementioned scenario.

- How will this feedback impact on their working relationship with DC Adair?
- Do you also think it has the potential to impact on the reputation of the team as PC Whitlock was on attachment?
- How could the feedback be improved upon?
- Do you know how you best receive feedback?

Feedback approaches

Despite the aforementioned considerations this chapter has yet to be able to provide you with a golden approach to giving feedback. The reality is there is no such approach, but as with the rest of the book, hopefully a few of the following options will resonate with you.

Within policing the utilisation of a certain type of sandwich is often advocated; however, in the book *Radical Candor* it argued that sandwiching meant that some of the messages got lost and the positives were insincere (Scott, 2018, p 21). Considering the aim of feedback is to make a marked improvement, it could be argued that the overuse of the sandwich has meant that it loses its impact and original intention. What follows is several different approaches you could use in your practice, which could mean avoiding the use of the good, bad, good sandwich.

Seven steps to feedback

In Nottingham and Nottingham's title *Challenging Learning through Feedback* (2017, pp 121–34), the book culminates in the model outlined in Figure 8.1, the seven steps to feedback. This title is clearly written with a classroom in mind so within a policing context it is evident that this model cannot be used everywhere as it advocates re-writes and time and space to reflect, which is not always possible. However, for tasks such as writing their own statement, casefile building or other skills often taught in initial training and conducted within the station or office, this approach could be good to help drive up standards. This could also work for those who are doing an apprenticeship and need to write essays, a skill which does not always come naturally for everyone.

Figure 8.1 A summary of the seven steps to feedback

Agree learning goals	Draft	Self/peer review
• For students to be able to understand their progress and frame their feedback they must understand the standards they are being assessed on.	• This stage involves the student 'doing' whatever activity may be required of them.	• This stage is important as it builds a self-assessment skillset, but by understanding stage 1, they should be able to review one another's work.

Edit	Teacher feedback	Complete
• Given the above feedback this is the student's opportunity to make corrections.	• At this stage this is your opportunity to intervene and provide some guidance. Which you may have done so already.	• This is the student's opportunity to take your feedback onboard and make changes. The authors argue it's bizarre that feedback is often given once the task is complete.

Grade
• Sometimes grades can be arbitrary but an acknowledgement of the progress made could be sufficient.

Stop, start, continue

Stop, start, continue aims to break feedback down into three easy-to-use steps:

1. Stop – What practice would you like them to stop doing?
2. Start – What suggestions do you have for their practice?
3. Continue – What is being done well which you want to keep seeing?

Breaking feedback down into these three easy sections makes it punchy, able to identify areas of good work, provides constructive suggestions and hopes to stop bad practice early.

When it comes to making improvements, one study, based on university course feedback, found that the use of these headers meant that the comments made were significantly more constructive, meaning that how to make the improvements was included naturally within the body of all three questions. If you compared it to a question which asked about the 'best thing', whilst helpful in that it provided feedback that was explained, it did not provide ideas on how to make it better. The study goes further to describe that even when students were given an opportunity to write free text to provide feedback, over 80 per cent of what was given was either descriptive or qualified in comparison with when provided with the same free text task but given the stop, start, continue template this was reduced to less than 40 per cent (Hoon et al, 2014).

In a policing context, the stop, start, continue model is practical; it can be as drawn out as required but provides structure in a useable format. Its ability to encourage more constructive comments will be more beneficial for the learner and naturally due to the format limits endless pieces of feedback and therefore gives the learner some direction. It would be more challenging in a group feedback setting such as when there is more than one learner to educator and they all need feedback at the same time. Starfish feedback, detailed later on, might be a way to overcome this, which is similar but allows all the participants to take part.

REAL-LIFE POLICING

You are tutoring PC Wilson, who has just conducted their first video-recorded interview with a victim. Understandably there were some nerves in the first interview and PC Wilson was over-analysing their performance. You did not think it was that bad and want to celebrate the good bits but also need to highlight areas for development to ensure they grow without damaging their confidence too much.

As such you opted to use stop, start and continue feedback. You informed PC Wilson that they need to stop using leading questions and you utilised an example in the interview where PC Wilson asked for more information on the blue car when the victim had not mentioned the colour. You stated that they need to start looking at the victim's body language to consider whether they need a break and finally you finished by saying they need to continue with their great rapport with the victim, which they built up with the victim prior to the interview, as this made the interview much less stressful for them.

This made PC Wilson realise that they had the basis of a good interview but to still focus on clear areas of development.

Starfish feedback

The starfish feedback builds on the previous approach but simply provides two more questions to answer, detailed later on. This means that if you have to provide feedback to more than one person in a group setting, everyone can be given these headings to look at and discuss.

Figure 8.2 Starfish feedback, based on Kua (2006)

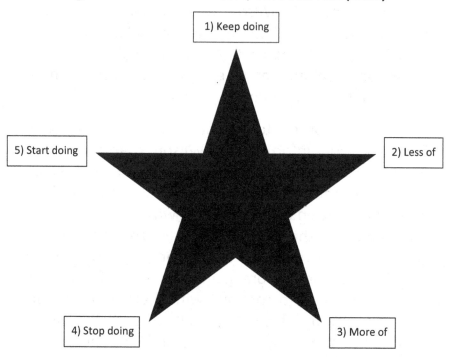

To avoid repetition, the three questions from the previous model will not be explained, but we focus on the two new headings.

- Less of – this helps highlight the practice which did not work or requires refinement. It could be that the method they used was still of some help but yet not enough to spend time on it next time they come across a similar situation. An example of this kind of discussion could be when it comes to investigating crime and what an officer in charge might decide what is or is not a reasonable line of enquiry. A tutor on review might consider the enquiries taken differently.

- More of – this is a bit of the practice you want to highlight you would like to see more often. In a group feedback session this is a great way to highlight practice others could adopt. An example of this could be in a public order situation when someone deals with what is presented well. If others had done the same, the situation could have been resolved quickly.

This feedback, if presented on paper, can be more visual for those that prefer that and can also be great discussion points for group sessions. Whilst this book is aimed at supporting students you may also find this approach helpful when debriefing with a team and it has been argued to be able to raise performance whilst still encouraging collaborative work (Van Aert, 2024). What could be a challenge with this model is ensuring that everyone understands the headers to ensure the same comments are not repeated as this would be frustrating to the learner and limits the tools impact. Additionally, whoever is the lead facilitator in a group feedback setting must make a great effort to avoid a 'pile-on' to one candidate. If something has gone slightly wrong, it is quite easy to blame an individual when policing is a team job and usually there is someone else who could have intervened.

AID feedback

The final model this chapter discusses is AID feedback. This feedback approach can be used as a conversational guide with an individual and would work best in a one-to-one situation. This model strips out the why people have done a particular task as, whilst this can be important in other contexts when wanting to alter behaviour, understanding the consequences of actions can be more impactful. AID stands for:

- **A**ction;
- **I**mpact; .
- **D**esired outcome.

Action

Action is about describing what took place, what was done, what was seen and the evidence base. This section in essence is about setting the scene for the provision of feedback. The key here is to be precise and not allow extra information which clouds the description of the act.

Impact

Having completed the first stage, the next element is about discussing what the impact of this action was. This is often missed out and can add more impact to the person receiving the feedback rather than them getting defensive. This impact can also be quite broad. Consider not just the evidence but also the potential impact on the police reputation and any additional work colleagues have needed to do. If you know the individual you could encourage them to self-reflect on this element and then add any additional points.

Desired outcome

This section is about the 'what next?'. Having set out the action and the impact, the learner should be in a good position to be able discuss next steps and this element should at least in the first instance be a discussion driven by them. It could be discussing the action and impact of a certain element that worked really well and needs to continue, but equally it can be that a practice needs to change due to its unintended consequences (Pearce, 2021).

This model is particularly good when you are tutoring someone who is still discovering the role. Self-reflection as discussed in the managing performance chapter is a powerful tool and this model encourages this and allows you as the person supporting them to build on it. Importantly it also strips out the why someone did something. Whilst this might be helpful for the learner to justify their actions, this model ultimately focusses on the outcome which is often the focus of the public when it comes to police attendance.

SUMMARY OF KEY CONCEPTS

This chapter has discussed a range of topics in regard to feedback.

- Feedback is clearly important. Davenport has described the consequences of not giving it, including tolerating poor performance, which also frustrates the wider team.
- Dahl et al explained six key considerations when giving feedback.

  1. Timing.

  2. Content form and mode.

  3. Frequency.

---

4. Relationship.

5. Specificity and level of support.

6. Individual traits.

- There are a range of different approaches to give feedback, not all of which will work in each setting or for each learner. This chapter has discussed:
  o The seven steps to feedback, which is an approach that allows the learner several opportunities to review, alter and correct their work prior to final submission. This model is particularly good if they have the time and space to reflect and receive feedback at different times;
  o Stop, start and continue is an approach which provides three clear headers for the feedback providers to really focus on, both the good and bad of a particular task at hand;
  o Starfish feedback builds upon the previous model, however, it is advocated to be better in group settings. The additional two headings allow for more granular feedback, picking up elements of practice which could be tweaked but would not necessarily be picked up in the previous model;
  o AID feedback stands for Action, Impact and Desired outcome. This model is a way of having a conversation with students and breaking down the impact, whether intended or not, of their actions and then understanding the next steps.

NEXT STEPS IN PRACTICE

Giving feedback is an art and is something that will require experimentation to find what works for you and your learner. That said, however, by considering the following you will hopefully put yourself in a great position to give feedback to your learners.

- Understand your learner and how you feel about a given situation before you provide feedback. Many of the six key considerations will be heavily influenced by these factors.
- As with all policing tasks, not one approach will work for all situations. Be aware of the different feedback approaches and in which circumstances they generally thrive best. Having a toolbox of approaches will make this process easier and make you less reliant on one approach.
- Be prepared to get feedback on your feedback! Feedback is not a one-way street and you may be a potential expert in the original task; however, you are not the expert on how your feedback impacted on the individual. Sometimes you will only really understand someone when you make a few mistakes, so listen to what they say, learn and adapt your approach accordingly.
- Know how your particular organisation records feedback. Especially in someone's early career there are often formalised processes for recording what took place. These are important – if you stop supporting them, the new person can do so from an informed place if they know what you said before.

Further reading

Kilgallon, M and Wright, M (2024) *Behavioural Skills for Effective Policing: The Service Speaks.* St Albans: Critical Publishing.

This title is a collection of articles from different authors on some of the key behavioural skills in policing. Whilst certainly less hand-on than this title, the list of authors have a range of policing experience and provide interesting insights alongside case studies.

The Open University (nd) *Applying Psychology to Work.* Available at: www.open.edu/openlearn/applying-psychology-work (accessed 16 January 2025).

The OpenLearn website has a range of CPD opportunities for you to use, including topics on policing, psychology and the legal system. However, for this chapter the section on applying psychology to work is particularly helpful. The content given is not particularly scientific but is presented in a way that lets you understand best evidence without feeling confused about what you read! This section on the website has loads of information which I believe would be highly useful to both those who support students and those who supervise.

Part 3

Police specifics

Introduction to Part 3

The final part of this book is what really makes this title different from any other book about supporting students, albeit up until now with a policing twist! It much more specifically addresses some of the issues faced by those supporting policing students on the frontline.

The current make-up of policing in England and Wales means that many within the service will not have as much experience as previous generations of police officers. This is not to say that these individuals would not be as efficient at being coaches, in fact, some will probably be better qualified! However, what it does mean is that some may not be exposed to various circumstances or be present when both them and their student experience their first incident/ court or other element of policing. This section hopes to highlight some key considerations in the more popular areas. As such, it is not intended to be the ultimate guide to each area; some chapters have entire specialist books dedicated to that topic, but it is hoped that by taking on board at least some of the advice you will be heading in the right direction.

Chapter 9 starts this section with information about dealing with domestic abuse. This is for anyone who has been in or around policing for any length of time; it is a key area for policing to get right and also an area in which a poor response can be disastrous. This chapter helps explain some of the complexity in this ever-growing area as well as some common mistakes policing has previously made in relation to dealing with domestic abuse cases to ensure you can guide your students well.

The following chapter, Chapter 10, deals with death. Regardless of whether you are a PC, DC or police staff it is highly likely you will both encounter death and potentially investigate it. This chapter helps you know how to best support your student through what can be an emotive time for both the deceased family and the students themselves.

Chapter 11 moves on to what can be a nerve-racking time for any person in policing regardless of your level of experience, which is attending court. TV has dramatised the experience somewhat and the buildings themselves are intimidating in their own right. In a circumstance where potential tutors, mentors or coaches may never have attended courts themselves, this process can be even more intimidating. In reality, however, court can be both interesting and develop you as an investigator – you just have to navigate the nerves and some of the language used! This chapter helps explain the courtroom and provides some tips for good preparation so that even if you lack experience in this area you can still offer some advice.

The final chapter of this book discusses the National Investigators' Exam (NIE). This exam is mandatory for anyone wishing to become a detective or PIP2 investigator. Historically most of those supporting candidates would have been based in those core investigative departments such as CID; however, with the emergence of specialist entry routes this is becoming less likely. Supporting students through this exam having had no prior experience can be very difficult, therefore, this chapter helps explain some common pitfalls and some advice you can provide to students.

Finally, I hope this book has been of some help to you, and I wish to finish the book with how I started, by saying thank you for all that you do.

Chapter 9

DEALING WITH DOMESTIC ABUSE

CONTENT WARNING

Domestic abuse can affect anyone, including those within policing. As a result, this chapter may resonate particularly strongly with certain readers. Please ensure that you are aware of the support which may be available to yourself, within your organisation, or elsewhere.

It can be difficult to ask for help from people you know or may have to see at work. Further advice and guidance is available here:

www.citizensadvice.org.uk/family/gender-violence/domestic-violence-and-abuse/.

You may find the Bright Sky app useful, recommended on GOV.UK (GOV.UK, 2023), details of which are available here:

www.hestia.org/brightsky.

LEARNING OBJECTIVES

After reading this chapter you will be able to:

- describe the importance of dealing with domestic abuse correctly;
- understand some of the complexities of dealing with domestic abuse;
- reflect on how these can make the policing response difficult.

Introduction

Domestic abuse (DA) is, rightly, a priority for policing. The crime survey for England and Wales estimated that there are 2.1 million different victims of domestic abuse who are aged over 16 years old, and the vast majority of victims are women (1.4 million) compared to men who made up 751,000 (Office for National Statistics, 2023). This number is huge and whilst the police recorded number is far below the true number, it still creates a significant amount of demand for policing, which in turn creates particular challenges for the workforce to address when responding. Alongside this volume, however, policing must also acknowledge the importance of getting its response right. In the year up to March 2023, there were 100 domestic homicides; this is the lowest it has even been since electronic records began (Office for National Statistics, 2024), but yet still represents just under 20 per cent of all homicides. Failure to deal with these incidents, therefore, can have tragic consequences.

Your job as someone who supports students is to understand these issues and ensure that you yourself do not portray any of these issues whilst acting as a role model to the students who could be young in service. Equally, if you see them naturally occur then you should be in a position to challenge to ensure high levels of service.

A note before starting

Domestic abuse is a complex area and there are entire books dedicated to the subject. Therefore, this chapter cannot and will not explore all the intricate details which an officer should know. Additionally, it is worth highlighting that due to its greater prevalence the guidance, support and research surrounding domestic abuse is naturally tilted towards female victims; this does not make male victims any less important – if anything it makes it sometimes harder to find them support as a result. This fact should be kept in mind when reading this chapter as the research could exclude a certain demographic; this does not make the research less valuable but a factor to bear in mind.

Finally, there was consideration to include in this chapter violence against women and girls (VAWG) and it can be argued that this is by far the more topical area in policing. Considering the earlier discussion, domestic abuse clearly influences some of the work done in VAWG. However, VAWG is broader, encompasses a broad range of behaviours and as a result could not be discussed sufficiently in this chapter. In addition, the work around it is constantly evolving, so by focussing this chapter on a topic not yet really established the book risked being out of date before publication. Again, this is not to diminish the VAWG agenda but to ensure that this title remains focussed and in date to assist you in your practice.

REFLECTIVE PRACTICE 9.1

As an individual who works or has a key interest in policing:

- What is your understanding of domestic abuse?
- What are your personal frustrations with dealing with domestic abuse?

What is domestic abuse?

Different organisations and charities have varying definitions on what makes up domestic abuse, which can create its own particular issues. However, the cross-government definition of domestic violence and abuse is:

> *Any incident or pattern of incidents of controlling, coercive, threatening behaviour, violence or abuse between those aged 16 or over who are, or have been, intimate partners or family members regardless of gender or sexuality.*

(College of Policing, 2021)

This is a clearly broad definition and its broadness is intentional; what may make up domestic abuse in one relationship could be entirely different in another. This definition is designed to ensure that as many behaviours by as many perpetrators are captured within the definition whilst still providing a core definition of a defined behaviour type.

You will notice that this chapter opts for domestic abuse over violence, unless specifically utilised in another source.

This is intentional as violence can be seen to be somewhat narrow and exclude behaviours which are worth including in order to build up a whole picture.

The complexities in domestic abuse and the police response

Unlike many offences which take place in the public arena and therefore have a plethora of other witnesses or lines of enquiry, DA often takes place behind closed doors, meaning the evidential picture when it comes to criminal justice outcomes can be more difficult. Over time, evidential rules have been implemented to assist with this challenge but the high threshold for a criminal conviction remains.

DA by its very nature has the victim and the suspect emotionally connected, in a way where often the victim may not wish to get the other into trouble or they may be too scared of the repercussions to do so, whether that be from the perpetrator or the personal strain that having the other excluded may put on them. This puts them in an impossible position, despite the fact that the police are expected to both manage the risk, seek criminal justice outcomes where needed and engage with the victim and suspect. A study which helps explain the complexities of victim decision making found that the victim's main concerns were:

- seriousness of the offence/dangerousness of the offender;
- costs of co-operation;
- likelihood of conviction.

Whilst the first and third points are straightforward, the costs of co-operation are much broader than people often consider at first glance and as such are split into two categories.

1. Tangible costs – cost of time lost from work, loss of income from the household etc.
2. Reputational costs – this is the belief that others will view them as blameworthy or culpable in the victimisation (Kaiser et al, 2015).

From a police response perspective and when coaching students through a domestic deployment, sharing an understanding of these key decision points can help both your students' and your approach towards victims.

The complexity in police being able to select the right response in the eyes of the victim is best illustrated in a study in America which asked victims how they felt about the police response to their call. In this study around one third regretted calling the police, 22 per cent wanted the offender arrested but they were not and in 23.8 per cent of the cases the offender was arrested when the victims did not want it. On a positive note, however, the vast majority of 69.7 per cent of victims stated they would call the police again (Johnson, 2007, pp 505–7). What this collection of statistics shows is that there is no single 'right' response to domestic abuse in the eyes of the victim, and officers acting in line with policies may in turn negatively influence the victim's perception of the police. We should also consider, given the various factors influencing victim decision making, that policing may have to make a decision which the victim would never agree with.

Outside of the victim perception, some studies add to this idea of there being no correct approach. The 'pro-arrest' approach is often argued in the belief that arrest, and consequently prosecution, reduces violence, but this on its own does not, and will only have an impact when it forms part of a wider package of social interventions (Hoyle and Sanders, 2000). Equally, if policing goes down the 'victim choice' route there is a chance that due to coercion and other pressures victims are not protected from risks.

Police areas to develop in the response to domestic abuse

As with all complex areas of policing, the response from the police has not always been perfect and given the nature of this type of offence, there are unique difficulties that attending officers should be aware of. As a policing mentor, being aware of these issues and being able to explain and guide those new in service is of vital importance to ensure that a high-quality response is consistently provided.

Due to the complexities involved with domestic abuse, one of the common types of casefile used are evidence-led, which means that they are done without the victim's account in statement form. These prosecutions are harder, as often we have a victim account but via a third party, which means that additional rules of evidence apply. But learning from these cases will help improve the policing response. Despite this, however, feedback between both CPS and policing is limited. A recent joint inspection report between CPS and policing stated that good work and successful outcomes should be shared with their teams (Criminal Justice Joint Inspection, 2020, p 20); but yet despite the report, this is not always the case. A recent HMICFRS report stated that it has noticed marked improvements in the response to VAWG offences, including use of body-worn video, better identification of repeat victims and committed and professional responses (HMICFRS, 2021). This progress, however, is only successful if its practice is continued. As someone supporting trainees this can be implemented in your practice. Without doubt, you will have experience in knowing what works and how evidence-led prosecutions can be maximised; part of your role is not just about showing the individual how to navigate the process, but also impart your wisdom of how to produce the best outcomes for victims.

Another key issue is attending officers' attitudes. Research has shown that this has massively improved since the 1980s; however, officers still represent societal views and as such until society can adjust its opinion and outlook on domestic abuse then views perpetuating around in the public will continue to influence the police workforce and in turn, police attendance. One author argued that police culture is masculine and consequently this influences the police response to gendered-based crimes such as domestic abuse. It does, however, go on to argue that this area would require extra research as it is not currently explored enough (Carrillo, 2021). This issue is, however, an important one to be aware of when it comes to supporting students; given the volume of calls it could be quite easy for officers to become dismissive or 'victim fatigued', and as someone who is supporting students it is up to you to help keep these students on track and deliver a professional response to all calls for service.

The final issue this chapter discusses is regarding the attending officers' understanding of risk. One study that looked at officers from both the UK and US found that despite attending officers being aware of the range of factors involved in the risk assessment to adequately assess risk, officers still often relied on a select few to decide the final risk level, and the majority of these were around physical violence. Whilst those who had received training were more likely to view the coercive control elements as important it still was not adequately considered (Robinson et al, 2016). It is expected that all new recruits would receive this training; however, amongst the noise of other training it is easy for the important issues to get lost, especially if we consider the culture mentioned in the previous paragraph.

One model which highlights the importance of these other factors is the homicide timeline by Professor Jane Monkton-Smith, in her book *In Control: Dangerous Relationships and How They End in Murder* (2021). She sets out and explains eight key stages which takes the perpetrator from the early stages of a relationship, triggers, escalation, change in thinking, right through to death in the end of the most serious of cases.

IN CONTEXT

PC Rod was in their eighth week of their response attachment. Towards the end of their shift they get a report for their third domestic abuse call of the night. It is reported as a verbal only, with a neighbour reporting it. In this particular set of shifts PC Rod has already attended this address twice and they are aware that other units have also attended over the same period.

On hearing this call, PC Rod turned to his tutor and says *'Again? Can they not just sort their own arguments*

$\rightarrow$

out between themselves?' This was not questioned by their tutor. On arrival, PC Rod sits down with the victim and was at first dismissive with them and the victim went on to explain that nothing had happened. The tutor then asks the victim about the concealer she is wearing around her eye; the victim goes to wipe it away and revealed a black eye. The victim then goes on to discloses a series of assaults over the last month and that during the previous police attendances she never disclosed it as she felt the attending officers were not interested. She then revealed bruises all over her body. She did not want to provide a statement but did not feel safe in her own home.

The officers captured the disclosure on their body-worn video, took photos of the bruising and did house-to-house with a neighbour providing a statement saying that they regularly hear arguing, the victim rarely leaves the house, has no visitors and they only see the perpetrator leave. The attending officers provide a statement covering the disclosure and the victim's demeanour. On arrest, the suspect says, *'No comment'* but the CPS make the decision to charge the perpetrator with battery.

The domestic abuse team review the previous occurrences and the body-worn video from the other attendances and end up providing reflective practice to the attending officers on how they treated the victim. They also noticed that the domestic risk assessment was graded as standard, which meant many had not been reviewed yet. On proper review of the BWV and the risk assessment, they should have been graded as medium and as such further support would have been given to the victim.

REFLECTIVE PRACTICE 9.2

Dealing with domestic abuse can take its toll. Reflect on the aforementioned scenario.

- How will you ensure that your students will attend each domestic abuse professionally?
- Victim fatigue is a real issue in policing. Have you ever noticed yourself or a colleague providing a diminished service as a result?
- Going forward how will you check in with yourself or colleague to prevent it impacting service delivery in the future?

SUMMARY OF KEY CONCEPTS

In this chapter the following has been discussed.

- Domestic abuse has a broad definition; this is intentionally so to capture the broad number of behaviours perpetrators use.
- Domestic abuse is difficult to police; victims are understandably emotionally intwined with the perpetrators. Plus there are a number of other considerations they need to make before committing to filing a report.
- Despite evidence-led prosecutions being a mainstay of domestic abuse prosecutions, sharing of lessons in their creation does not take place as often as it could.
- Police attitudes to attending domestic abuse have been described as poor.

$\rightarrow$

- Police understanding of risk can be patchy. This means that too much weight is often put on violence rather than other concerning behaviours.

NEXT STEPS IN PRACTICE

- Are you confident of the key factors to consider when it comes to risk? Does your force have any guidance on this?
- Do you know what 'good' looks like when it comes to evidence-led prosecutions? Equally do you know what makes a poor one?
- Are you aware of the training students get when it comes to domestic abuse?

Further reading

College of Policing (2021, October 25) *Context and Dynamics of Domestic Abuse*. Available at: www.college.police.uk/app/major-investigation-and-public-protection/domestic-abuse/context-and-dynamics-domestic-abuse (accessed 16 January 2025).

It is hard to find a singular easy-to-understand and police-focussed resource on domestic abuse. However, the College of Policing in the APP makes a good attempt. It covers definitions, first responses, protection orders, investigative steps and victim safeguarding all in one place. For any officer, this resource should already influence your policing practice.

Monkton-Smith, J (2021) *In Control: Dangerous Relationships and How They End in Murder*. London: Bloomsbury Circus.

I read this title when it was newly released, and I sang its praises then. It is easy for officers to take a tick-box approach to safeguarding; however, this book explains the key steps of progression a perpetrator can take and does so in an easy-to-follow model. Whilst this book is based upon academic rigour, it does not feel so and therefore I strongly recommend it to anyone attending domestic abuse incidents.

Chapter 10

DEALING WITH DEATH

LEARNING OBJECTIVES

After reading this chapter you will be able to:

- understand some of the impact of dealing with death;
- understand the common criticisms faced by policing around death;
- be aware of well-being plans to help support your student.

Introduction

Dealing with death is an inevitability when it comes to policing, whether it is due to a crime, or a sudden or unexpected death which requires investigation. Despite your knowledge of first aid, you will come across death in policing, even if you are not an officer. Death is not simply about dealing with a deceased body; policing has a broad involvement, including scene searches (including the body), conducting investigations, attending coroner's court, and informing and liaising with the family. As with all facets of policing, naturally you will have some who excel at various elements of this; however, policing must be professional in its response to death, which includes looking after ourselves and our colleagues.

It is also important to realise that our responses to death and each different circumstance are individual and sometimes the same scenario can impact different people in unique ways. As a tutor of multiple students, you may encounter challenges in which you may need support. Couple that with new officers who understandably are afraid to make a mistake or clearly struggle to emotionally handle policing, and this particular challenge becomes even harder for those supporting them.

REFLECTIVE PRACTICE 10.1

Talking about death can be difficult. As with all activities only engage with this if you are emotionally able to and ensure you have adequate support around you.

- Do you remember your first interaction with death?
- Does this interaction differ to the first time you dealt with death in a policing context?
- Is there anything you wish new officers knew that you could share with them?
- How did you find talking about it afterwards? If you did not, why did you not talk about it?

The impact of death

An individual's exposure to death will vary based on district and role. As an example, I would expect British Transport Police officers to attend more 'one under' deaths than say, those that take place in a home. Consequently, their tolerance levels to different types of incidents will vary. Scenes in themselves can also be an assault on the senses, which, if individuals are not prepared for or not expecting, can be difficult. In one article scenes were described as containing:

> More often than not there's a trail of shit throughout the house, somebody's over the toilet bowl and there's vomit everywhere.
>
> (Carpenter et al, 2016, p 307)

I have heard throughout my service a wealth of different approaches to help cope with the smell and the scene presented to you, and whilst I am not sure any of them have been robustly tested, strong-smelling alcohol-based hand sanitiser under the nose worked well for me.

It is worth noting that exposure to death throughout someone's career is also not evenly distributed. Henry (2004, pp 26–7) highlights that, *'rookie [recently graduated police officers] officers tend disproportionately to receive these assignments'* and as such receive a *'baptism of fire'* when it comes to sudden deaths. As someone who supports students you will need to ensure that this tranche of work is constructive, meets the needs of the service and is not overwhelming.

Each death is unique; however, as discussed in previous chapters, early discussions en route to a call and explaining the process may help alleviate a student officer's nerves. Remember that even a 'routine death' is likely to remain with a student officer for some time and the build-up to it can be worse than the actual attendance. A little reassurance and guidance at an early stage can help calm the nerves.

As with a lot of policing, attending death well still comes down to people skills, and the police criticisms of such skills will be discussed later on. Using these skills also has an impact on those dealing with the incident. As an example, one officer was quoted as saying:

> *I found going to scene emotionally draining because of the family members being there.*
>
> (Carpenter et al, 2016, p 306)

As a tutor, you do not have to just help an officer deal with an incident, but you also need to help equip them to be able to tackle such a situation and do so professionally. To help with the post-incident, well-being plans discussed at the end of this chapter may be beneficial.

Understanding police criticism

An SIO was asked what a successful murder investigation was, and his response was:

> *It would be easy to just say a conviction, wouldn't it? But it's not really that, it's a bit more than that, I suppose it's keeping as many people happy as much of the time as possible.*
>
> (Brookman and Innes, 2013, p 292)

Although this quote is aimed at homicide investigations it is applicable to all death investigations, and can apply to both the family, witnesses and our colleagues. Much of the criticism over time also relates to the police's approaches and occasions where this has gone wrong.

Child death in particular can be particularly difficult to approach. This is the worst emotion to experience as a parent yet despite this the police have a role to play to ensure that there are no circumstances that warrant further criminal investigation. This work must be completed at a time when these emotions are raw and probably at their highest, therefore the response from policing must be professional and compassionate. In one piece of research into Māori families and SIDS (Sudden Infant Death Syndrome), a family member described the police response:

> *they were more frightened...I feel for those cops being chucked in at the deep end. That's when things start to go all wrong.*
>
> (Clarke and McCreanor, 2006, p 32)

This is clearly not an ideal impression to leave family members, and equipping students to deal with such situations is key to your role in supporting them and the family. As a result, in some situations it may be beneficial to be more task-based towards your student(s), followed by a proper learning debriefing, so in the future they can take control of the incidents.

Another concern often raised is regarding 'gallows humour' especially when dealing with traumatic situations. Joking has been described as *'vital to the performance of such serious jobs and negotiations of the emotional burdens associated'* (Vivona, 2014, p 128). However, it is important to note that the same article also states that others find such jokes to be of poor taste, and this is an important lesson for a student officer to learn. I was often taught in my initial stages: *'imagine the chief constable was in the room'*, and this is a good steer to appropriate behaviour, especially in public. But discussions with students about gallows humour and understanding both the right place, right time and right audience is vital especially if it is seen as a normal coping mechanism. I mention in another book, *Criminology and Crime Prevention* (2024), that every contact leaves a trace, and the public's perception of the police can be based on a singular interaction. This is hyper-focussed when around death, as emotions can often be high and the attending police, unfortunately, can often be the foci of frustrations and upset.

Looking after your students

Looking after students is vital. In one study, an increased level of on-the-job stressors was linked to increased dissociative symptoms (Aaron, 2000), which are both unhelpful for the student to learn and for the public they serve. The National Police Wellbeing Service, Oscar Kilo, provide a fantastic range of resources available for those who may need support for a range of well-being reasons, supervisors who support them and force-wide guidance. Another advice page which has a range of resources that are easy to print is available via Police Mutual (Police Mutual, nd), a link of which is available in the further reading section.

As a result, I strongly recommend being cognisant of what advice and guidance is available should you need it either personally or as a tutor.

When it comes to traumatic incidents, Oscar Kilo advises that talking to colleagues in a debriefing can be helpful to allow people to organise what happened in their minds, which can in turn reduce feelings of helplessness (Oscar Kilo, nd). As a tutor, this debriefing process probably comes quite naturally to you and is often done in an informal way during most incidents, especially in the early stages of tutoring. However, when going to a traumatic incident, such as death, it may be good practice to ensure a suitable debrief takes place with those involved and you find time to do so.

The College of Policing themselves have provided comprehensive guidance on responding to trauma in policing. Whilst this echoes a lot of what has been discussed earlier, it does also highlight that psychological responses and interventions to stress and trauma should be followed up to ensure staff are improving, and if not other interventions should be considered (College of Policing, 2018, pp 12–13). This is where knowing what is available to you and how to access it is important.

Wellness support plans

A great concept is wellness support plans (WSP). These are individualised plans owned by the person they relate to, where they can share what 'well' looks like for them, what type of work environment suits them best, the coping strategies they already use and what does not work for them.

Essentially this guide provides you, them and your supervisors with the information needed to both monitor their well-being and take steps to intervene if needed.

This can be used as a template for potential one-to-ones between you and your student and also empower you to know how best to speak to your student should they show signs that they may be struggling (Cambridgeshire Constabulary, nd). A great WSP template has been shared on the Oscar Kilo website from Cambridgeshire Constabulary; however, your organisation may have their own.

IN CONTEXT

Police Staff Investigator (PSI) Lightfoot has joined a prisoner handling team as a trainee. During their initial learning and development review, their tutor explains the wellness support plan and provides the form to PSI Lightfoot to complete.

PSI Lightfoot brings the plan to their next meeting, and they discuss their wellness in depth.

As PSI Lightfoot comes to the end of their probation they are assaulted during an interview and are visibly shaken up. Their supervisor and tutor conduct a debrief with them. In the following weeks, the tutor does not notice a visible improvement and discusses it with the supervisor. PSI Lightfoot and their tutor have a one-to-one session and discuss the well-being support plan again and they highlight their concerns. A package is then put together for PSI Lightfoot, and over a period of time improvements start to be seen.

REFLECTIVE PRACTICE 10.2

Having conversations about someone who is struggling can be difficult. Imagine you were in that position.

- What would you want from that conversation?
- What could be the worst thing someone could say to you at that time?
- How would someone else know what to say to you?

SUMMARY OF KEY CONCEPTS

This chapter has looked at police involvement in death.

- Police criticism has been broad in the response to death; however, professionalism in your and your student's approach will go a long way.
- It is important to remember that death presents itself in a myriad of ways and what might affect one person will not affect another, and vice-versa.

- Knowing what can support your student is vital. You may not know the answers but knowing who might will make your practice a lot easier.
- Wellness support plans can help you approach the difficult topic of well-being and enable you to have a constructive conversation before an issue arises.

NEXT STEPS IN PRACTICE

- Are you confident in your force's policies and procedures for dealing with death, including child death and criminal investigations which often have different responses?
- Do you know if your force has wellness support plans? If they do, how do you approach them and store the information?
- Can you recall the support available to staff in your force? If not, do you know where to go for advice? Especially if you work nights where there are less available people around to ask for advice.

Further reading

Cambridgeshire Constabulary (nd) *Guideline for Managers: Wellness Support Plans (WSPs)*. Available at: www.oscarkilo.org.uk/media/467/download?inline (accessed 16 January 2025).

This guide from Cambridgeshire Constabulary is fantastic at explaining the purpose, the effectiveness and how to use a wellness plan. In addition it is not academic and as such, presented in a way that anyone can read and use.

Oscar Kilo (nd) *Wellbeing Toolkit*. Available at: www.oscarkilo.org.uk/resources/toolkits-and-campaigns/wellbeing-toolkit (accessed 16 January 2025).

Oscar Kilo is a fantastic resource which continually expands its offering. The wellbeing toolkit is a great place to look if you wish to try something new, whether that be that your current approaches are not working or if you think there might be another better option. It also provides contact details for those in service who have previously implemented practice so you can make contact.

Police Mutual (nd) *Wellbeing Hub*. Available at: www.policemutual.co.uk/activity/wellbeing/ (accessed 16 January 2025).

Before writing this chapter, whilst I knew Police Mutual provide assistance, I was not aware of the level or extent! If you have a colleague who needs advice, this is a broad resource and a good one to have in your arsenal of ideas.

Chapter 11

GOING TO COURT

LEARNING OBJECTIVES

After reading this chapter you will be able to:

- know how to support someone who is going to court;
- understand what to expect when giving evidence;
- provide advice for those attending court.

Introduction

Going to court can be a scary thought, but those who work within policing the public, policing internally and the courts expect us to be able to tackle the court experience with the minimum of fuss and to a good standard.

As someone who supports students this can also put pressure on you to not only maintain those high standards for yourself, but also to ensure they are met by the individual(s) you are supporting. This can be difficult when you may not have been to court yourself or only have limited experience. This chapter hopes to guide you through the process and point you in the direction of additional resources should you need it.

This chapter focusses on crown court appearances. Whilst the majority of cases are dealt with in the magistrate's court, due to the nature of volume crime the hearings are fleeting and there are no juries in such trials. Crown court, however, is usually where the more serious cases go and where the most anxiety rests. That said, the skills are still able to be translated.

The courtroom

Each courtroom is laid out slightly differently, so it is difficult to provide a go-to 'this is what a court room looks like'. However, they do tend to follow the same rules.

Figure 11.1 Basic layout of a courtroom, adapted from Victim Support (nd) and Fitzpatrick (2006, p 88)

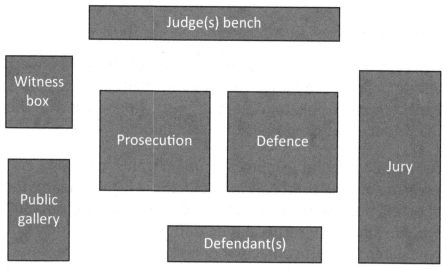

As you can see from Figure 11.1, the judge(s) will sit in the most prominent place in the room, usually under the crest of the court service. Following that, the defence barristers will be between the prosecution and the jury, in order to fend off the allegations of the prosecution in a somewhat symbolic manner. The witness box is where everyone will give their evidence, including the defendant if they opt to do so, and is generally opposite the jury or somewhere prominent, meaning the jury and judge can clearly see, as it is vital that they can see any witness give evidence, even those with special measures.

If you or the person you are supporting gets an opportunity before trial, I strongly recommend going into the courtroom your trial is due to be heard in and have a look, as it removes one unknown element. Courtrooms often open earlier in the morning before the daily business begins, so that is an ideal opportunity. Visiting the courtroom earlier also give you an opportunity to introduce yourself to the court usher, who ensures the smooth running of the courtroom. These individuals are the hidden heroes of the courtroom and if you ever need a favour to help with the trial (such as photocopying, finding a witness in the building etc), they will usually know someone who can help, so being friendly towards them pays huge dividends. They also know timings, what other hearings are going on and any potential issues. As the officer in charge of the case, knowing all this information can be helpful to you to keep the witnesses updated and manage your tasks on the day.

How to prepare

When you attend court often it will be either as an officer in charge (OIC) of an investigation or as a witness in the case. Regardless of your role the key to success is preparation. You have been called to provide a piece in the case and therefore knowing the relevant information to your role will make your experience a lot smoother.

As an OIC I would recommend having the following prepared. Whilst this information should have already been supplied to the CPS it does not hurt to have the material to hand, especially if the prosecution cannot locate it, which can happen surprisingly often:

- physical copy of the casefile, including printed copies of statements and exhibits;
- witness contact information and knowledge of what time they are attending court;
- knowledge of the casefile, key bits of evidence and defence case statement and how your evidence may address some of the points raised.

Having this prepared means that should you have any last-minute requests or changes to timetables you will be in a strong position to deal with them with ease. Please remember that due to the way the criminal justice system operates, the reviewing barrister in the case may not be the individual who presents the case in court, so issues previously raised may crop up again. Whilst frustrating, it is certainly easier to deal with a known issue than one which you have not heard of before!

Also as an OIC on the first day of the trial, it does not hurt to be friendly to those involved, including the defendant and their legal representation. Your role as an investigator is to follow all reasonable lines of inquiry which both point towards and away from the defendant; as a consequence you have to interact with everyone! Being friendly makes this process easier and if any challenges are likely to appear, you may just be told about them earlier rather than them being sprung upon you in the witness box!

If you are there as a witness, I strongly recommend reading your statement(s); typically without leave of the court you are not able to read it in the witness box. As a result, being able to recall your statement can make the experience easier and save you having to get permission to read it, not to mention the pressure of having to read it with so many people watching!

If you have used any particular powers, especially if the use could be controversial, regardless of whether you think it is right, it will be strongly beneficial to ensure you revise that particular power or law so if you get any questions about it, you will be in a good position to answer adequately and look professional in front of a jury. These areas of controversy may be the 'in' the defence use to question the quality of your evidence, and as such knowing your stuff can fend off an early challenge.

Giving evidence

Giving evidence in its basic form should not be complicated. The whole role of the individual being a witness is to relay the facts as they know them, and the barrister's role, regardless of which side they sit on, is to test those facts and get the most accurate version of events.

Despite that, however, officers frequently get shown up in court, and the following tips are bits of advice I would share with policing students to help them survive.

- Answer the question and the question only – generally these are being asked for a particular reason and the questions are going somewhere. Do not try and provide extra information or be clever, as this is where people often get tripped up. If a yes or no will suffice that is all you need to say.

- Speak clearly, focussing your answers towards the judge and jury. Whilst the barristers ask the questions, the ones assessing the quality of the evidence are the jury and the judge. I was always told to point my feet towards the jury, this way when you naturally turn to the barrister when they speak, your body will always want to face those that need to see you.
- Do not get frustrated, this is a defence barrister's dream. You are a professional and we are also human, so if you make a mistake own it and move on. But frustration shows weakness and might invite pressure.
- Do not be afraid to disagree. Sometimes a barrister will ask a few questions where you agree and kind of lead you down the garden path. Listen to each one and if necessary disagree. Remember, you are a witness and they are present to test your account, so if you think a statement from them is incorrect, say so and if need be explain why.
- Take a breath. It is really daunting talking to a courtroom of people. But if you take a second have a breath, glass of water and slow your speech down, you will present yourself in a much better light and feel more in control of the situation.
- Finally, be prepared. In the box in most cases in policing, it is just you. Regardless of how hard a time you are getting, it is unlikely someone will rescue you. Unless the judge or counsel (barrister) thinks it is unfair, preparation can make this experience easier.

IN CONTEXT

Trainee DC Foley has their first trial in crown court for GBH. They have had this case from its early stages until now. During the preparation of the case, in line with the required schedules, the defence made a disclosure request which was responded to via the CPS within the agreed timescales.

As the trial drew closer DC Foley prepared a copy of the casefile, reviewed the defence case statement which mentioned the use of a special warning and questioned its appropriateness. As a result they revised the key legislation in regard to the special warnings which they used in interview.

On the first day of the trial, the prosecution barrister entered the police room and asked to speak to DC Foley. They had a very irate defence solicitor who claims to have never received a response to their disclosure requests. DC Foley provides the information and the proof that this was supplied to the CPS for the defence to review.

In trial DC Foley is asked to explain the role of the investigator, recite the caution, explain what it means, read the interview transcript, all of which is common practice, and was asked questions about the special warning, which the defence claimed was inappropriately applied. DC Foley, aware of the legislation, was able to confidently explain what the law said to the jury and explained why it was relevant. Having made this explanation, the defence had no further questions to ask and they did not have to be cross-examined for extended periods.

REFLECTIVE PRACTICE 11.1

Imagine you were DC Foley.

- How would you have coped about questions about special measures if you had not prepared?
- Imagine you are coaching DC Foley. How would you help them manage their preparation?
- What key factors do you think have a bearing on the jury's perception of DC Foley's evidence?

SUMMARY OF KEY CONCEPTS

This chapter helped explain some of the key pieces of knowledge when it comes to attending court.

- Police witnesses regardless of their experience are expected to have a higher level of competence in the court arena.
- Courts have a range of people present, all with different roles. It is important to understand who is who and how you should interact with them.
- Preparation is key for court attendance. Even if you have a smaller role, understand your powers and why you did what you did.
- Know in advance how to present your evidence and speak to the prosecution barrister if you need advice.

NEXT STEPS IN PRACTICE

- Have you been to your local court and can you explain to your student the layout?
- Are you confident in giving evidence?
- Do you know who you could speak to for support or guidance on the court process? (If you do not, I suggest an experienced DC may be a good contact.)

Further reading

Barrister, S (2019) *Secret Barrister: Stories of the Law and How it's Broken*. London: Picador.

A slightly different recommendation, insofar that this is by no means an academic book. However, what it does do is show the realities of working in the court system and certainly helps demystify the process that many barristers go through when preparing a case. This title is the first in a series and I strongly recommend reading them, both to help you with your job and they are also quite an amusing read.

Fitzpatrick, B (2006) *Going to Court*. Oxford: Oxford University Press.

Having written the majority of this chapter, I referred to this book to ensure that what I was saying was both correct and I did not miss anything out. Having read it, despite being a slightly older title it presents information about court attendance both in more detail than a singular chapter can afford and in a really easy format. I would strongly recommend getting hold of this title if I were to either present evidence in court or support someone through the process.

Chapter 12

THE NATIONAL INVESTIGATORS' EXAM

Introduction

The National Investigators' Exam (NIE) is an essential element to becoming a detective and seeks to test the knowledge expected from a detective or PIP2 investigator. Historically it was an exam which was taken by more experienced officers looking to become detectives. However, due to the rise of specialist entry routes to becoming a detective and police staff even if you are not a detective yourself you may find yourself in a position where you need to support someone through the exam!

This chapter does not explain the syllabus to you as it evolves too regularly for that to be of benefit. However, what it does do is empower you to know about the exam, how to support your student and hopefully along the way it may also improve your legislative knowledge. This exam is hard and understandably so – as a result, any candidate will not only require support but also self-investment to get through. Passing first time is achievable, however, especially if they start early and take into account the following advice.

The exam

The College of Policing operate the NIE in a similar way to promotion examinations (NPPF Step 2 exams) and the exam is taken online.

The NIE consists of 80 multiple choice questions which must be completed within two hours, or more if the candidate has reasonable adjustments. Despite the candidate having to answer 80 questions, only 70 will count towards the score with the 10 worst performing questions removed. At the time of the exam there is no way of knowing which questions will be removed from the scoring so they must all be treated in equal measure.

It aims to test the candidate in four key areas.

1. General principles, police powers and procedures.
2. Serious crime and other offences.
3. Property offences.
4. Sexual offences.

The exact contents of the syllabus is in the most up-to-date copy of Blackstone's Police Investigators' Manual and this is the official textbook for the exam (College of Policing, 2022). It is published around November time every year for the following year's exam to ensure it has the most up-to-date content.

Common mistakes in the exam

The following common mistakes are from my personal experience of doing the exam, receiving advice from others about the exam and finally guiding others through the exam. Clearly this list is not exhaustive but hopefully will keep you on the right track.

Using 'street' law

Part of your work with a student may involve converting the knowledge they have gained from initial training and converting it into usable practice, accepting that whilst training is good there are some clear differences between what is taught and its application. For those unaware of this difference, a comparison between the law on assaults and CPS charging standards are a clear illustration.

The NIE, however, uses the law 'as is' in a black-and-white world where charging standards simply do not exist. This therefore means that when training a student, you must make the distinction clear and if there is a conflict, encourage your student to research using their materials to ensure they know what is needed for the exam.

IN CONTEXT

It is getting close to the exam and PC Abara has only just started their revision. In a panic they opt not to read the non-fatal offences chapter, as they deal with assaults all the time and get charges successfully from CPS, meaning they must know the law.

$\rightarrow$

On the day of the exam there is a question about what amounts to battery. PC Abara answers according to charging standards unaware that according to Blackstone's, the injury sustained is technically an ABH.

When PC Abara gets their exam feedback they are confused as they trust their tutor and the CPS that the charges given were correct.

Only knowing surface level detail

Only knowing surface level detail is a challenge when it comes to the exam, especially for those who leave initial training feeling like their legislative knowledge is enough. When overcome, this level of knowledge is a good thing for ensuring quality detectives, as knowing the law well can help them make quick and effective decisions. But for those preparing for the exam, it breeds overconfidence in particular areas which candidates often use in their day job, resulting in them overlooking these areas because 'they already know it'.

As an individual supporting someone through their NIE, I strongly recommend looking at the chapter on theft in the Blackstone's Police Investigators' Manual (Connor et al, 2022). As an officer or support staff you will be confident in the definition of theft if you use it every day. However, it will soon become clear whilst reading that chapter that whilst you understand theft, you probably do not understand the depth of knowledge needed for the NIE. If you do, congratulations, but even if you have previously revised for an exam, your knowledge may well be out of date by now.

REFLECTIVE PRACTICE 12.1

- Prior to reading the chapter on theft, how confident were you in your knowledge?
- On reading it, how much did you realise you did not know?
- What were your thoughts on the manual; is the content accessible?
- What could you do to make it more accessible for your student?

The NIE goes far beyond those initial definitions that most people know from training and looks at the detail that you would expect a detective to know when they are attending an incident or an officer goes to them for advice. As a result the NIE tests difficult areas such as case law and the key note sections of the manual (although the questions can come from anywhere in the manual). In regard to case law the little stories used in the questions are practically already written, making it easy content to examine! As a result, it is important for the student to understand the fine grain detail, otherwise they simply will not pass the exam.

As someone who supports students it is important that you do not let them rest when you know they have a similar knowledge to yourself. Push them to engage with the content and know the detail required to pass the exam. This can be done by asking what-if questions after a job or pushing them to exhibit their legal knowledge when the opportunity arises.

Only using questions to revise

There are a multitude of question banks available to purchase, see later on for a list of available resources, to assist candidates through the exam. These helpful tools, however, are by their very nature limited as to the breadth of content that they cover. On occasion it has been known for students to focus solely on questions on the premise that if it is in a question bank it might come up in the exam. However, question writers are creative people and base their content on the manual and as such by not using it (or any other product derived from it) exclusively or near exclusively means that the candidate risks limiting their exposure of the full curriculum. Whilst they are most certainly an effective and useful tool they should not be used in isolation.

Personally I have heard a number of candidates tell me that '*X question bank was nothing like the exam*', and it is important to remember they are not supposed to be; they are intended to highlight key content and indicate how they could be presented in an exam.

As someone who supports students, use this to your advantage; set them tasks to read content and then if you have access to questions, test them using the questions, or if you hear of poor practice correct them and explain why.

Supporting your student

If you have not done the exam or NPPF exam yourself, supporting your student through it can be difficult. However, there are a number of ways you can assist especially now you are aware of the common pitfalls students make.

Link the NIE to work

In some deployment situations, especially if you work in a rural area, there may be some time between being deployed to the incident and actually arriving at the scene. In Chapter 2, research showed that having those pre-arrival conversations was valued by students, therefore the NIE allows you to put this into practice. From your experience you will know likely offences they could come across, so why not ask the student about them? It is a practice which might push their working knowledge at first; however, if you come back to areas, they are likely to start retaining knowledge.

Hold students to account

Students are busy people; they will have competing demands between learning their role, potential academic work and studying for the NIE. When conducting your one-to-ones with the students or even in casual conversation, ask them what their plans are and then follow up another day. This casual check-in will create that little voice in the back of their mind when they are tempted not to stick to the plan. When it comes to plans for revision, ensure they are varied; simply reading the book or just doing the questions is probably not the most effective method, and having read previous chapters you may be in a position to suggest other methods of revision.

That said, however, students are also human beings. Please ensure they have time away from revision as 24/7 studying is neither healthy nor effective.

Find them opportunities

Finding opportunities to study is not just about finding them time, although I am sure they will be appreciative of that.

But you can be creative in other ways; briefings could be a good time to upskill an entire team about legislation used in a recent incident they attended. If this is linked to the NIE it forces the student to engage with the content and produce it in a presentable format.

Equally if there is a CPD opportunity about a topic in the exam, encouraging them to consider attending might not only help their work, but also bring some of the information they read to life.

I have been told of students being sent on longer distance prisoner transport runs to allow them time to read and revise – being creative is key.

Encourage them to share

This partially links to the previous section, but by getting a candidate to talk about what they have learnt they have to engage with the content and understand it. Sometimes this can be as simple as talking about a topic in briefing, but ensure you give them adequate time to prepare. Or if you know they are writing up notes, have a look at them!

There are various technical options to encourage this on a candidate-to-candidate level. If you have a messaging software that can handle team or group chats, you could put those studying the NIE together. They can ask each other questions, share their troubles and also share their notes. Studying can be a lonely place at times so by allowing them to share, you are allowing them not to be isolated and borrow ideas from others, whilst also accepting on a practical level that you cannot always have them in the same room together.

External support available

Table 12.1 highlights a range of products available on the market to help support students through the NIE. None of these are personal recommendations as I have not had interactions with all of them, but I have been spoken to about them with some level of positivity. It is also worth highlighting that what works for one student may not work for another, and many of these offer a free trial or sample so it may be worth sending your student to look at their options.

Table 12.1 NIE support sources

Company	Service(s) offered and link
Checkmate Training	Two-day NIE crammer course – this company is probably the most well-known within policing and is known to have some of the authors of the Blackstone's textbook present so they do know the content well. www.checkmatetraining.co.uk/.
Police Pass	Textbooks, e-learning, crammer course and multiple-choice question banks are on offer. Police Pass offer a one-stop shop for NIE learning and students can tailor what they purchase to their needs. I have heard good things about the e-learning and crammer courses and the manuals distil a lot of the nonsense in Blackstone's to a product which is much easily digested. www.police-pass.co.uk/.

$\longrightarrow$

Table 12.1 (Continued)

Company	Service(s) offered and link
Julianna Mitchell Training	Audio guide – I have personally used this product and would recommend it. Julianna distils the manual into an audio file which you can play in your car, on the go etc. Driving to and from work is where this product really shines as you can revise whilst commuting. www.jmitchelltraining.co.uk/.
Police Revision	Guidebook, video presentations, multiple choice question bank and workbooks. Police Revision are newer to the market but offer a range of items in a singular package. Students I have spoken to seem to rate this company. www.policerevision.com/.
Anthony Turner	Anthony Turner is relatively new to the market and does not have a website that you can go to. However, he does have a YouTube page with free questions you can listen to (search: AnthonyTurner.NPPF-NIE) and has a range of books available on Amazon, which, compared to others, are reasonably priced.

SUMMARY OF KEY CONCEPTS

- The NIE contains key areas of law from police powers to offence legislation.
- It is based on law 'as is' so it is important to not get confused with charging standards.

- It is important to ensure that students utilise a mix of revision techniques. Solely utilising one method will not help.

NEXT STEPS IN PRACTICE

- Are you aware of your students' plans to revise?
- Do you know what areas of law come up in the exam?
- How will you hold them to account?
- What support does your force provide?

Further reading

College of Policing (2022) *National Investigators' Examination (NIE) Candidate Handbook 2023*. Ryton: College of Policing.

I would strongly recommend ensuring you are aware of the latest College of Policing guidance when it comes to the exam. This is the most up to date at the time of writing (October 2023). Included in the College of Policing guidance are also areas, which, whilst appearing in the manual, due to changes or typing errors they have opted not to include within the exam. As such this could save your student valuable reading time!

Connor, P (2024) *Blackstone's Police Investigators' Manual 2025*. Oxford: Oxford University Press.

This book is the sole official textbook for the exam, and as such if I were referring anyone to find a question in relation to the exam it would be here. I was once told that if it's not in the book it will not be in the exam, and that is an important fact to remember when fielding questions. If you also like having a reference book, this is a good one to have as it covers large areas of the law that police frequently use. The criticism often levelled at it, however, is that the language is not the most accessible, so be prepared for an academic read! Also you will note that the 2025 version is referenced. Please note the manual is updated and published around November time every year, so make sure you study from the correct manual!

REFERENCES

Aaron, J D (2000) Stress and Coping in Police Officers. *Police Quarterly*, 438–50.

Antoniuk, A (2019) Learning Styles: Moving Forward from the Myth. *Canadian Journal for New Scholar in Education*, 85–92.

Babakr, Z H, Mohamedamin, P and Kakamad, K (2019) Piaget's Cognitive Developmental Theory: Critical Review. *Education Quarterly Reviews*, 517–24. doi:10.31014/aior.1993.02.03.84.

Bates, B (2019) *Learning Theories Simplified.* London: Sage.

Bayley, H, Chambers, R and Donovan, C (2004) *The Good Mentoring Toolkit for Healthcare.* Abingdon: Radcliffe Publishing.

Beehr, T A, Ivanitskaya, L, Hansen, C P, Erofeev, D and Gudanowski, D M (2001) Evaluation of 360 Degree Feedback Ratings: Relationships With Each Other and With Performance and Selection Predictors. *Journal of Organizational Behaviour*, 775–88. doi:10.1002/job.113.

Beersdorf, W W (2018) Meeting Individual and Organizational Wellness Needs. Available at: https://leb.fbi.gov/articles/perspective/perspective-law-enforcement-wellness-meeting-individual-and-organizational-needs (accessed 16 January 2025).

Bell, C R and Goldsmith, M (2013) *Managers as Mentors: Building Partnerships for Learning.* San Francisco: Berrett-Koehler.

Blackbyrn, S (2023) *Coaching Models: STEPPA.* Available at: https://coachfoundation.com/blog/models-steppa/ (accessed 16 January 2025).

Bonebright, D A (2010) 40 Years of Storming: A Historical Review of Tuckman's Model of Small Group Development. *Human Resource Development International*, 111–20. doi:10.1080/13678861003589099.

Boon, B (2015) *Blackstone's Leadership for Sergeants and Inspectors.* Oxford: Oxford University Press.

Brett, J F and Atwater, L E (2001) 360° Feedback: Accuracy, Reactions, and Perceptions of Usefulness. *Journal of Applied Psychology*, 930–42. doi:10.1037//0021-9010.86.5.930.

Brierley, J (2022) Developing a Learning Culture and Environment. In Kilgallon, M and Wright, M (eds) *Behavioural Skills for Effective Policing: The Service Speaks* (pp 235–54). St Albans: Critical Publishing.

Brookman, F and Innes, M (2013) The Problem of Success: What Is a 'Good' Homicide Investigation? *Policing and Society*, 292–310.

Brown, G, Leonard, C and Arthur-Kelly, M (2016) Writing SMARTER Goals for Professional Learning and Improving Classroom Practices. *Reflective Practice.* doi:dx.doi.org/10.1080/14623943.2016.1187120.

Buser, T, Gerhards, L and Van der Weele, J J (2016) Measuring Responsiveness to Feedback as a Personal Trait. *Tinbergen Institute Discussion Paper.*

Cambridgeshire Constabulary (nd) Guideline for Managers: Wellness Support Plans (WSPs). Available at: www.oscarkilo.org.uk/media/467/download?inline (accessed 16 January 2025).

Carpenter, B, Tait, G, Quadrelli, C and Thomason, I (2016) Investigating Death: The Emotional and Cultural Challenges for Police. *Policing and Society*, 698–712.

Carrillo, D (2021) Police Culture and Gender: An Evaluation of Police Officers' Practices and Responses to Domestic Abuse. *Journal of Global Faultlines*, 69–80.

Casey, B (2023) *An Independent Review Into the Standards of Behaviour and Internal Culture of the Metropolitan Police Service.* London: Metropolitan Police Service.

Cassidy, S (2004) Learning Styles: An Overview of Theories, Models and Measures. *Educational Psychology*, 419–44.

Cesoedes, F V (2022) How to Conduct a Great Performance Review. Available at: https://hbr.org/2022/07/how-to-conduct-a-great-performance-review (accessed 16 January 2025).

Chamberlin, J (2011) Who Put the 'ART' in SMART Goals. *Management Services*, 22–7.

Champathes, M R (2006) Coaching for Performance Improvement: The 'COACH' Model. *Development and Learning in Organizations*, 17–18.

Charman, S, and Tyson, J (2024) 'In the "Too Difficult" Box?' Organizational Inflexibility as a Driver of Voluntary Resignations of Police Officers in England and Wales. *Policing: A Journal of Policy and Practice*, 1–9. doi:https://doi.org/10.1093/police/paad104.

Chartered Management Institute (2011) Setting SMART Objectives Checklist. Available at: https://cdn.learn.civilservice.gov.uk/packages/NgoKaq_VS4yrAWPSSX1mTw/jdVhe-qYR9uo-XNgN4f_EQ/Setting%20SMART%20objectives.pdf (accessed 16 January 2025).

Clarke, E and McCreanor, T (2006) He wahine tangi tikapa...: Statutory Investigative Processes and the Grieving of Maori Families Who Have Lost a Baby to SIDS. *Kōtuitui: New Zealand Journal of Social Sciences Online*, 25–43.

Clutterbuck, D (2008) What's Happening in Coaching and Mentoring and What Is the Difference Between Them? *Development and Learning in Organizations*, 8–10.

Coffield, F, Moseley, D, Hall, E and Ecclestone, K (2004) *Learning Styles and Pedagogy in Post-16 Learning: A Systematic and Critical Review*. London: Learning and Skills Research Centre.

College of Policing (2015) Leadership Review. Available at: https://assets.college.police.uk/s3fs-public/2021-03/cop-leadership-review-2015.pdf (accessed 16 January 2025).

College of Policing (2016) Competency and Values Framework for Policing. Ryton: College of Policing. Available at: https://profdev.college.police.uk/competency-values/ (accessed 16 January 2025).

College of Policing (2018) *Responding to Trauma in Policing: A Practical Guide*. Available at: https://assets.college.police.uk/s3fs-public/2021-02/responding-to-trauma-in-policing.pdf (accessed 16 January 2025).

College of Policing (2021) Context and Dynamics of Domestic Abuse. Available at: www.college.police.uk/app/major-investigation-and-public-protection/domestic-abuse/context-and-dynamics-domestic-abuse#domestic-abuse-definitions (accessed 16 January 2025).

College of Policing (2022) *National Investigators' Examination (NIE) Candidate Handbook 2023*. Ryton: College of Policing.

College of Policing (2023a) Leadership Standards. Available at: www.college.police.uk/career-learning/leadership/leadership-standards (accessed 16 January 2025).

College of Policing (2023b) Code of Practice for Ethical Policing. Available at: www.college.police.uk/ethics/code-of-practice-ethical-policing (accessed 16 January 2025).

College of Policing (2024) Ethical Policing Principles. Available at: www.college.police.uk/ethics/code-of-ethics/principles (accessed 16 January 2025).

College of Policing (nd) Beyond 360° Feedback Tool. Available at: www.college.police.uk/support-forces/beyond-360 (accessed 16 January 2025).

Connor, P, Johnston, D, Hutton, G, Cox, A, Gold, E and Parry-Davies, S (2022) *Blackstone's Police Investigators' Manual 2023.* Oxford: Oxford University Press.

Counselling Tutor (2022) The Skilled Helper Approach. Available at: https://counsellingtutor.com/the-skilled-helper-approach/ (accessed 16 January 2025).

Cozens, P (2008) Crime Prevention Through Environmental Design in Western Australia: Planning for Sustainable Urban Futures. *International Journal of Sustainable Development and Planning*, 272–92. doi:10.2495/SDP-V3-N3-272-92.

Criminal Justice Joint Inspection (2020) *Evidence Led Domestic Abuse Prosecutions.* Available at: www.justiceinspectorates.gov.uk/cjji/wp-content/uploads/sites/2/2020/01/Joint-Inspection-Evidence-Led-Domestic-Abuse-Jan19-rpt.pdf (accessed 16 January 2025).

Cuevas, J (2015) Is Learning Styles-based Instruction Effective? A Comprehensive Analysis of Recent Research of Learning Styles. *Theory and Research in Education*, 308–33.

Dahl, O, Damen, M-L, Bjørkelo, B, Meling, C P and Jensen, M R (2023) The Role of Verbal Peer Feedback in the Police: A Scoping Review. *Vocations and Learning*, 227–50. doi:https://doi.org/10.1007/s12186-023-09316-z.

Davenport, S (2022) Challenging Conversations. In Kilgallon, M and Wright, M (eds) *Behavioural Skills for Effective Policing: The Service Speaks* (pp 99–120). St Albans: Critical Publishing.

De Haan, E and Gannon, J (2016) The Coaching Relationship. In Bachkirova, T, Spence, G and Drake, D (eds) *The Sage Handbook of Coaching* (pp 195–217). London: Sage.

Drago-Severson, E and Blum-DeStefano, J (2017) *Tell Me So I Can Hear You: A Developmental Approach to Feedback for Educators.* Cambridge, MA: Harvard Education Press.

Egan, G (2002) *The Skilled Helper: A Problem-Management and Opportunity-Development Approach to Helping.* Pacific Grove, CA: Brooks/Cole.

Ehrich, L C, Tennent, L and Hansford, B C (2002) A Review of Mentoring in Education: Some Lessons for Nursing. *Contemporary Nurse*, 253–64.

Feldstein, M and Hill, P (2016) Personalized Learning: What It Really Is and Why It Really Matters. Available at: https://er.educause.edu/articles/2016/3/personalized-learning-what-it-really-is-and-why-it-really-matters (accessed 16 January 2025).

Fitzpatrick, B (2006) *Going to Court.* Oxford: Oxford University Press.

Flaherty, J (2005) *Coaching: Evoking Excellence in Others.* Burlington: Elsevier.

Fletcher, S J (2012) Coaching: An Overview. In Fletcher, S and Mullen, C A (eds) *SAGE Handbook of Mentoring and Coaching in Education* (pp 24–40). London: Sage.

Gage, N L and Berliner, D C (1991) *Educational Psychology.* Boston: Houghton Mifflin.

Gardiner, C (2003) Mentoring: Towards a Professional Friendship. In Downie, C M and Basford, P (eds) *Mentoring in Practice: A Reader* (pp 79–86). London: University of Greenwich.

George, M, Lim, H, Lucas, S and Meadows, R (2015) Learning by Doing: Experiential Learning in Criminal Justice. *Journal of Criminal Justice Education*, 471–92.

Goldner, L (2008) The Quality of Mentoring Relationships and Mentoring Success. *Journal of Youth and Adolescence*, 1339–50.

Gould, J (2012) *Learning Theory and Classroom Practice in the Lifelong Learning.* Exeter: Learning Matters.

GOV.UK (2012) FOI Release: Definition of Policing by Consent. Available at: www.gov.uk/government/publications/policing-by-consent/definition-of-policing-by-consent (accessed 16 January 2025).

GOV.UK (2023) Domestic Abuse: How to Get Help. Available at: www.gov.uk/guidance/domestic-abuse-how-to-get-help (accessed 16 January 2025).

Grimley, B (2020) *The 7Cs of Coaching: A Personal Journey Through the World of NLP and Coaching Psychology.* Abingdon: Routledge.

Grimley, B (2022) The 7Cs of Coaching and Therapy. In Yousefi, H R (ed) *Jahrbuch Psychotherapie – NLP – In Practice: Internationale Zeitschrift für PsychoPraxis* (pp 57–70). Nordhausen: Verlag Traugott Bautz.

Groff, J S (2017) *Personalized Learning: The State of the Field and Future Directions.* Boston: Centre for Curriculum Redesign.

Guney, A and Selda, A (2012) Effective Learning Environments in Relation to Different Learning Theories. *Procedia-Social and Behavioral Sciences*, 2334–8. doi:0.1016/j.sbspro.2012.05.480.

Hardy, S.-J, Chakraborti, N and Cuko, I (2020) More Than a Tick-box? The Role of Training in Improving Police Responses to Hate Crime. *British Journal of Community Justice*, 4–20.

Harvard Business School (2004) *Coaching and Mentoring: How to Develop Top Talent and Achieve Stronger Performance.* Boston: Harvard Business School Press.

Henry, V E (2004) *Death Work: Police, Trauma, and the Psychology of Survival.* Oxford: Oxford University Press.

HMICFRS (2021) *Police Response to Violence Against Women and Girls: Final Inspection Report.* London: HMICFRS. Available at: https://hmicfrs.justiceinspectorates.gov.uk/publication-html/police-response-to-violence-against-women-and-girls-final-inspection-report/ (accessed 16 January 2025).

Hoel, L (2020) Police Students' Experience of Participation and Relationship During In-field Training. *Police Practice and Research*, 576–90.

Hoon, A, Oliver, E, Szpakowska, K and Newton, P (2014) Use of the 'Stop, Start, Continue' Method Is Associated With the Production of Constructive Qualitative Feedback by Students in Higher Education. *Assessment and Evaluation in Higher Education*, 1–13. doi:http://dx.doi.org/10.1080/02602938.2014.956282.

Hoyle, C and Sanders, A (2000) Police Response to Domestic Violence. *British Journal of Criminology*, 14–36.

Hughey, J (2020) Individual Personalized Learning. *Educational Considerations*, 46(2). doi:https://doi.org/10.4148/0146-9282.2237.

Huitt, W (2009) Humanism and Open Education. Available at: www.edpsycinteractive.org/topics/affect/humed.html (accessed 16 January 2025).

Hussain, I (2017) Pedagogical Implications of VARK Model of Learning. *Journal of Literature, Languages and Linguistics*, 33–7.

Huybrecht, S, Loeckx, W, Quaeyhaegens, Y, De Tobel, D and Mistiaen, W (2011) Mentoring in Nursing Education: Perceived Characteristics of Mentors and the Consequences of Mentorship. *Nurse Education Today*, 274–8.

Johnson, I M (2007) Victims' Perceptions of Police Response to Domestic Violence Incidents. *Journal of Criminal Justice*, 498–501. doi:doi.org/10.1016/j.jcrimjus.2007.07.003.

Johnson, R R (2012) Police Organizational Commitment: The Influence of Supervisor Feedback and Support. *Crime and Delinquency*, 1155–80. doi:https://doi.org/10.1177/001112871 2466887.

Johnson, S D, Suriya, C, Yoon, S, Berrett, J V and Fleur, J L (2002) Team Development and Group Processes of Virtual Learning Teams. *Computers and Education*, 379–93.

Jokelainen, M, Turunen, H, Tossavainen, K, Jamookeeah, D and Coco, K (2011) A Systematic Review of Mentoring Nursing Students in Clinical Placements. *Journal of Clinical Nursing*, 2854–67.

Kaiser, K A, O'Neal, E N and Spohn, C (2015) 'Victim Refuses to Cooperate': A Focal Concerns Analysis of Victim Co-operation in Sexual Assault Cases. *Victim and Offenders*. doi:10.1080/ 15564886.2015.1078864.

Kamarudin, M B, Kamarudin, A Y and Ramiaida binti Darmi, N (2020) A Review of Coaching and Mentoring Theories and Models. *International Journal of Academic Research In Progressive Education and Development*, 289–98.

Kanninen, E (2008) *Learning Styles and e-learning*. Tampere: Tampere University of Technology.

Karp, S and Stenmark, H (2010) Learning to Be a Police Officer: Tradition and Change in the Training and Professional Lives of Police Officers. *Police Practice and Research*, 4–15.

Kay, D and Hinds, R (2015) *A Practical Guide to Mentoring (5th edition)*. London: Robinson.

Kelly, C (1997) David Kolb, The Theory of Experiential Learning and ESL. Available at: http://iteslj.org/Articles/Kelly-Experiential/ (accessed 16 January 2025).

Kelly, J, Ellison, C and Burns, J (2023) David Carrick: The Serial Rapist and Abuser in a Police Uniform. Available at: www.bbc.co.uk/news/uk-64283783 (accessed 16 January 2025).

Kua, P (2006) The Retrospective Starfish. Available at: www.thekua.com/rant/2006/03/the-retrospective-starfish/ (accessed 16 January 2025).

Lawlor, K B and Hornyak, M J (2012) SMART Goals: How the Application of Smart Goals Can Contribute to Achievement of Student Learning Outcomes. *Developments in Business Simulation and Experiential Learning*, 260–7.

Leach, S (2021) Behavioural Coaching: The GROW Model. In Passmore, J (ed) *The Coaches' Handbook: The Complete Practitioner Guide for Professional Coaches* (pp 176–86). Abingdon: Routledge.

Leung, K-K and Weng, L-J (2007) Validation of Kolb's Structural Model of Experiential Learning Using Honey and Mumford's Learning Style Questionnaire. 醫學教育, 234–43.

London, M, Mone, E M and Scott, J C (2004) Performance Management and Assessment: Methods for Improved Rater Accuracy and Employee Goal Setting. *Human Resource Management*, 319–36.

McLeod, A (2004a) Performance Coaching and Mentoring in Organisations. *Resource Magazine*, 28–31.

McLeod, A (2004b) STEPPA Coaching Model. *Anchor Point*, 15–20.

McLeod, S (2018) Jean Piaget's Theory of Cognitive Development. *Simply Psychology*, 1–9.

Monkton-Smith, J (2021) *In Control: Dangerous Relationships and How They End in Murder.* London: Bloomsbury Circus.

Morgan, A, Cannan, K and Cullinane, J (2005) 360 Feedback: A Critical Enquiry. *Personnel Review*, 663–80. doi:10.1108/00483480510623457.

Morin, A (nd) Personalized Learning: What You Need to Know. Available at: www.understood.org/articles/personalized-learning-what-you-need-to-know (accessed 16 January 2025).

National Police Chief's Council and Association of Police and Crime Commissioners (2016) Policing Vision 2025. Available at: www.npcc. police.uk/SysSiteAssets/media/downloads/publications/policing-vision/policing-vision-2025.pdf (accessed 19 January 2025).

Nottingham, J and Nottingham, J (2017) *Challenging Learning Through Feedback.* Thousand Oaks, CA: Corwin.

Office for National Statistics (2023) Domestic Abuse in England and Wales Overview: November 2023. Available at: www.ons.gov. uk/peoplepopulationandcommunity/crimeandjustice/bulletins/domesticabuseinenglandandwalesoverview/latest (accessed 16 January 2025).

Office for National Statistics (2024) Homicide in England and Wales: Year Ending March 2023. Available at: www.ons.gov.uk/peoplepopulationandcommunity/crimeandjustice/articles/homicideinenglandandwales/yearendingmarch2023#trends-in-homicide (accessed 16 January 2025).

Oscar Kilo (nd) Wellbeing Toolkit. Available at: www.oscarkilo.org. uk/resources/toolkits-and-campaigns/wellbeing-toolkit (accessed 16 January 2025).

Pakpahan, F H and Saragih, M (2022) Theory of Cognitive Development by Jean Piaget. *Journal of Applied Linguistics*, 55–60.

Pearce, A (2021) Giving and Receiving Powerful Feedback. Available at:www.open.edu/openlearn/health-sports-psychology/psychology/giving-and-receiving-powerful-feedback (accessed 16 January 2025).

Pence, Z A and Snyder, K E (2017) Instruction Without Learning Styles: Possibilities and Promise. *Teaching for High Potential*, 17–18.

Police Federation (2022) Attrition Rates Show More Must Be Done to Retain New Recruits. Available at: www.polfed.org/news/latest-news/2022/attrition-rates-show-more-must-be-done-to-retain-new-recruits/ (accessed 16 January 2025).

Police Mutual (nd) Wellbeing Hub. Available at: www.policemutual.co.uk/activity/wellbeing/ (accessed 16 January 2025).

Potter, C (2015) Leadership Development: An Applied Comparison of Gibbs' Reflective Cycle and Scharmer's Theory U. *Industrial and Commercial Training*, 336–42. doi:10.1108/ICT-03-2015-0024.

Purswell, K E (2019) Humanistic Learning Theory in Counselor Education. *The professional Counselor*, 358–68. doi:10.15241/kep.9.4.358.

Rawson, G, Sarakatsannis, J and Scott, D (2016) How to Scale Personalized Learning. Available at: www.mckinsey.com/industries/education/our-insights/how-to-scale-personalized-learning (accessed 16 January 2025).

Riggall, S (2016) The Sustainability of Egan's Skilled Helper Model in Students' Social Work Practice. *Journal of Social Work Practice*, 81–93.

Robinson, A L, Pichevsky, G M and Guthrie, J A (2016) A Small Constellation: Risk Factors Informing Police Perceptions of Domestic Abuse. *Policing and Society*, 189–204. doi:https://doi.org/10.1080/10439463.2016.1151881.

Rogers, C (2008) *Leadership Skills in Policing.* Oxford: Oxford University Press.

Rogowsky, B A, Calhoun, B M and Tallal, P (2015) Matching Learning Style to Instructional Method: Effects on Comprehension. *Journal of Educational Psychology*, 64–78.

Rosewell, J (2005) Learning Styles. *Times Educational Suppliment*, 11–14.

Sangvigit, P, Mungsing, S and Theeraroungchaisri, A (2012) Correlation of Honey and Mumford Learning Styles and Online Learning Media Preference. *Computer Technology and Applications*, 1312–17.

Scott, K (2018) *Radical Candor*. London: Pan Books.

Sharlanova, V (2004) Experiential Learning. *Trakia Journal of Science*, 36–9.

Smith, J M (2020) Surgeon Coaching: Why and How. *Journal of Pediatric Orthopaedics*, 33–7.

Snook, B, House, J C, MacDonald, S and Eastwood, J (2012) Police Witness Interview Training, Supervision and Feedback: A Survey of Canadian Police Officers. *Canadian Journal of Criminology and Criminal Justice*, 363–72. doi:10.3138/cjccj.2011.E.13.

Staller, M S and Koerner, S (2022) A Case Example of Teaching Reflective Policing to Police Students. *Teaching Public Administration*, 1–16.

The University of Edinburgh (2020) Gibbs' Reflective Cycle. Available at: www.ed.ac.uk/reflection/reflectors-toolkit/reflecting-on-experience/gibbs-reflective-cycle (accessed 16 January 2025).

Timmins, F, Murphy, M, Howe, R and Dennehy, C (2013) 'I Hate Gibb's Reflective Cycle 1998' (Facebook©2009): Registered Nurses' Experiences of Supporting Nursing Students' Reflective Practice In the Context of Student's Public Commentary. *Procedia Social and Behavioural Sciences*, 1371–5. doi:https://doi.org/10.1016/j.sbspro.2013.10.046.

Torre, D M, Daley, B J, Sebastian, J L and Elnicki, M (2006) Overview of Current Learning Theories for Medical Educators. *The American Journal of Medicine*, 903–7.

Tuckman, B W (1965) Developmental Sequence in Small Groups. *Psychological Bulletin*, 384–99.

Tuckman, B W and Jensen, M C (1977) Stages of Small-group Development Revisited. *Group & Organization Studies*, 419–27.

University of Cumbria (2020) Gibbs' Reflective Cycle. Available at: https://my.cumbria.ac.uk/media/MyCumbria/Documents/ReflectiveCycleGibbs.pdf (accessed 16 January 2025).

University of Glasgow (nd) *Mentoring: Egan's Skilled Helper Model*. Glasgow: University of Glasgow.

US Department of Education (2017) *Reimagining the Role of Technology in Education: 2017 National Education Technology Plan Update*. Washington DC: US Department of Education.

Vaida, S E and Şerban, D (2021) Group Development Stages. A Brief Comparative Analysis of Various Models. *Psychologia-Paedagogia*, 91–110. doi:10.24193/subbpsyped.2021.1.05.

Van Aert, J (2024) Unlock the Power of Starfish Retrospective for Project Success. Available at: www.jelmar-van-aert.be/starfish-retrospective (accessed 16 January 2025).

Victim Support (nd) Guide to Crown Court (Criminal). Available at: www.victimsupport.org.uk/courtroom-support/index.php?page=courtroom (accessed 19 January 2025).

Vivona, B D (2014) Humor Functions Within Crime Scene Investigations: Group Dynamics, Stress, and the Negotiation of Emotions. *Police Quarterly*, 127–49.

Wieslander, M (2018) Marginalised Voice in the Inclusive Recruitment Discourse: A Dilemma of Inclusion/Exclusion in the (Swedish) Police. *European Journal for Research on the Education and Learning of Adults*, 61–77.

Winstanley, D and Stuart-Smith, K (1996) Policing Performance: The Ethics of Performance Management. *Personnel Review*, 66–84.

INDEX

Printed in the United States
by Baker & Taylor Publisher Services